Jⁿᵒ T. Lucas Junʳ Pinxt. Day & Son, Lithʳˢ to the Queen.

Faithfully Yours
Oliver J. Jones

London, Saunders & Otley

RECOLLECTIONS

OF

A WINTER CAMPAIGN

IN

INDIA:

IN 1857—58.

With Drawings on Stone from the Author's Designs,

BY

CAPT. OLIVER J. JONES, R.N.

LONDON STAMP EXCHANGE Ltd.

1989

Foreword to the 1989 Edition

In our security-conscious age, the idea of a private individual visiting the front line is a strange one. But the Victorians were much less sensitive about secrecy. In 1884, Captain Arthur Wilson of the Royal Navy won the Victoria Cross for his bravery at the Battle of El Teb, which he had attended merely as an onlooker. In 1856, Captain Oliver Jones demanded and was granted a year's leave which he then occupied by taking part in some of the fiercest fighting of the Indian Mutiny.

Oliver Jones joined the Royal Navy in 1826 at the tender age of 13 and was promoted lieutenant in 1839. At a time when many naval officers spent the majority of their time on half-pay, he managed to remain actively employed almost continuously; but without seeing any fighting. Then, within the space of five years, he took part in three different wars or campaigns at opposite ends of the world. In 1854/5 he was the Commander of the brand-new sail and steam wooden battleship HMS *Hannibal*, both in the Baltic and the Black Sea Campaigns of the Crimean War. In 1860, he commanded the paddle-steamer HMS *Furious* during the Second China War. In between, he found time to observe the fighting in India and – in that innocent era before the Official Secrets Act! to publish a most vivid and detailed account of the operation and of the forces involved.

Lucky for us that he did, for his *'Recollections of a Winter Campaign in India'* gives some fascinating insights into this most unhappy of Britain's colonial wars. Captain Jones was attached to the 53rd Regiment which meant that he had a front-seat view of the Relief of Lucknow by Sir Colin Campbell's force and his reminiscences are a rich source of information about the conduct of the campaign, seen with a professional's eye. His account of the assault on Lucknow itself is one of the best contemporary accounts we have of this confused battle.

Such insights would in themselves be sufficient to commend the book. But Jones seems also to have had an artist's eye for the unusual or picturesque aspects of the campaign. This emerges both in the marvellous illustrations, which are based on his own sketches, and also in the vivid descriptive passages. His accounts of the numerous Indian non-combatants, although marred by the unpleasant racial superiority of his generation, nonetheless create a very attractive and lively picture of these essential, and too often forgotten, participants.

However, to the naval historian, the most useful passages of all are those which deal with the undoubted 'stars' of the Lucknow operation: Captain Sir William Peel and the sailors of the Naval Brigade. Peel, portrayed here by a fellow-officer and an equal, emerges more vividly than in any of the other contemporary accounts. And Jones gives much fascinating detail about the minutiæ of the brigade's campaign: the special carriages that were devised for the *Shannon's* guns; the gun-sights; the horses 'moored head and stern'; the sailors' dress and marching – and their numerous pets! The mid-Victorian bluejacket comes to life again on Jones's pages, with all the characteristic cheerfulness, idiosyncrasy and resourcefulness which so endeared him to his contemporaries.

So Oliver Jones's *'Recollections'* are well worth reading; whether you are an historian or simply a lover of *Boys Own Paper* type stories of fighting men. You may not always like him: but you will never find him dull!

Colin White
Royal Naval Museum
January 1989

PREFACE.

When I returned home from India, I found that my friends had kept all the letters that I had written to them while in that country, and they joined in an united request to me to publish them, or to compile a book from them; and, though extremely averse to appear before the public as my own trumpeter, still their persuasions overcame the small remains of modesty which a great many years of battling with the world by sea and by land had left to a disposition originally, I fear, a little too prone to egotism.

I had also kept a journal, in which I had jotted down the daily occurrences, and whatever happened, that appeared to me remarkable and of interest.

My letters were written and sent with great regularity, and my journal was also as regularly kept, until my right hand was wounded, and rendered temporarily useless, when the journal was condensed into dates and places, and the letter-writing was reduced to a left-handed cacographical scrawl. From that time these pages became truly *Recollections;* and that must be my excuse for the meagreness of the details of the siege and capture of Lucknow.

I must beg the indulgence of my military friends for my descriptions of the battles, sieges, and operations—they merely profess to be the slight sketches of an uninitiated outsider; and I have only described the parts that I saw myself, or what was generally patent to the whole army.

Hundreds of instances of heroism occurred in them, of which I am unaware; and to many, things may appear different and from another point of view to that from which I have seen and described them.

It would require a far abler pen than mine to do justice to that army individually and collectively. I was prepared for much excellence, and to give it much admiration—to see great heroism, devotion, and bravery; but I was not prepared to witness such cheerfulness under toil — such uncomplainingness under privation—such zealous, ungrumbling discharge of the most onerous duties. I had not anticipated the unselfish way in which every one was ready to assist another, and to share his means and comforts with him how small soever they were. I did not expect to see such utter forgetfulness of self, such constant readiness for anything and everything to which duty and honour called.

I can only add, that my gratitude for the hospitality and consideration which I received from all—from Sir Colin Campbell down to the smallest drummer-boy of the 53rd—is only equalled by my admiration for him and the glorious army which he commands.

I have not filled these pages with suggestions as to the causes of the mutiny, as one writing about these momentous times might be expected to do: I had but small opportunity of forming a sound judgment of them. Not talking the language, I could have no conversation with natives who might have told me what they thought the reasons of it. Besides, in the daily march, the tented field, the battle's shock, one thinks much of the effects one sees—one speculates little on the causes which led to them. Nor, in the unsettled and disturbed state that affairs were then in, and from the few isolated and occasional facts which came under my observation, could I with any certainty discern the disturbing causes, which, for many years, had been at work, under the smooth but treacherous calm, which had wrapped India in fancied security, but which had at length burst forth in the almost irrepressible tempest which was raging around us. The sight may search many fathoms deep into the azure of the calm unruffled sea, but what eye can pierce the surface of the storm-heaved ocean—you may snatch a few snow-like foam-flakes from its dashing surge, but will they reveal what is passing in the unfathomed depth below? Still there are some things on the surface in characters so distinct, that "He who runs may read," clear as the handwriting on the wall at Assyria's monarch's feast—plain as their awful interpretation by the Prophet's denouncing voice. They are, "*that the seeds of the mutiny* were not sown by our *abuse of power*, but by the *want of the use of it.*"

That the growth of the mutiny was fostered not by severe and irritating discipline, but by its relaxation—by the discontinuing of the *lash* as a punishment for the *Sepoy*, while it was retained for that of the *British soldier;* by giving in to all the Sepoys' whims and fancies, reasonable or unreasonable; by trying to coax and cajole them to do their duty by rewards, often unmerited, instead of punishing the neglect of it: in fact, by allowing the performance of their duty to be a favour, instead of making it a necessity.

That the mutiny became ripe, and bore fruit, and *such fruit*, was not by any wrong, real or imaginary, put upon the Sepoy, but, that our treatment of them had made them cease to fear us, and to think that we feared them; that instead of our being their masters, they thought soon to be ours; and no wonder, when they saw disgraceful breaches of discipline, and, if accounts be true, *mutinies* slurred over, their officers blamed, themselves more pampered and petted; when they saw in the Gazettes their deeds (and the returns of killed and wounded show who bore the brunt of the fights), their behaviour, their valour put on a level with those of the British soldier (the latchet of whose shoe the Sepoy is not worthy to unloose), good reason had they to think we feared them, as we dared not even tell the truth about them; and when *the mutiny shall be repressed*, that the seed may not again fall into the ground, take root downwards, and bear fruit upwards—all this will not be accomplished by weak conciliation and *so-called mercy*. Mercy to the miscreant—injustice and cruelty to the peaceable, the well-disposed, the faithful—for upon how many innocent thousands, and tens of thousands, have these mutineers brought ruin, and desolation, and mourning, and woe? But they must be repressed by a stern, even-handed, certain justice; a justice that says, "the soul that sinneth (I mean the sins of murder, mutiny, and rebellion), THE SOUL THAT SINNETH, IT SHALL SURELY DIE."

CONTENTS.

CHAPTER I.
VOYAGE OUT — ARRIVAL AT ALEXANDRIA — RAILWAY FROM CAIRO ACROSS THE DESERT—SUEZ—CALCUTTA 1

CHAPTER II.
TRAVELLING IN INDIA — ARRIVAL AT BENARES — THE ENCAMPMENT 18

CHAPTER III.
BREAK UP ENCAMPMENT—MARCH TO ALLAHABAD—RAIL TO CHEMIE—MARCH TO FUTTEYPORE—CLEAR FUTTEYPORE DISTRICT 30

CHAPTER IV.
BITHOOR—THE NENA'S PALACE—TREASURE SEEKING—NAUTICAL ANECDOTE—KANONGE 47

CHAPTER V.
THE NAVAL BRIGADE — BATTLE OF KALA NUDDEE — FUTTYGHUR—THE ENFIELD RIFLE 59

CHAPTER VI.
AN EXECUTION—FURRUKABAD—INDIAN JUSTICE—RACES—A NIGHT EXPEDITION 87

CHAPTER VII.
RETURN TO HEAD-QUARTERS — ARRIVAL AT FURRUKABAD — AN INDIAN'S NOTION OF CHRISTIANITY—LIFE IN CAMP—MARCH TO CAWNPORE—A PIG-HUNT—ARRIVAL AT CAWNPORE—MARCH TO LUCKNOW—ARRIVAL OF MR. RUSSELL—CAMP-FOLLOWERS—RACES 109

CHAPTER VIII.

SKIRMISHING AT FUTTEYPORE—JAGGERMOW—BANGHURMOW—HEAR OF THE NANA—TAKING A "SHORT CUT"—STORMING OF MEANGUNGE—CAPTAIN STEWART—SCENES AFTER AN ENGAGEMENT 132

CHAPTER IX.

MONOA—A BRAHMIN BULL—MARCH TO LUCKNOW—SIR COLIN CAMPBELL—AN IRISH DISCOVERY—THE CUSHLA MAKREE OF THE KING OF OUDE—REACH LUCKNOW 146

CHAPTER X.

PREPARATIONS FOR THE SIEGE—THE DILKOOSHAH—MR. RUSSELL—PASSAGE OF THE GOOMTIE—THE BOMBARDMENT—SIR W. PEEL WOUNDED—THE ASSAULT OF LUCKNOW—SORTIE BY THE BESIEGED 157

CHAPTER XI.

ATTACK ON THE BEGUM'S PALACE—A SAD ACCIDENT—GALLANT CONDUCT OF A HIGHLAND PIPER—CAPTAIN MACBEAN—JUNG BAHADOOR VISITS SIR COLIN—ASSAULT THE IMAM BARA AND KAISERBAGH—ESCAPE OF THE MOULVIE 177

CHAPTER XII.

TURN HOMEWARD—MARCH TO CAWNPORE—LEAVE-TAKING—ARRIVAL AT FUTTEYPORE—ALLAHABAD—LOSE MY CAP—IMPROMPTU ONE—ROBBERY OF MALAKOFF—ARRIVE IN OLD ENGLAND 199

ILLUSTRATIONS.

	PAGE
PORTRAIT OF THE AUTHOR TO FACE TITLE.	
SHE SHIPPED SOME HEAVY SEAS	2
HYDRABAD MALAYAPEN, ALIAS MALAKOFF—SYCE NUNNOO	22
STARTING THE DAK GARRY	24
BREAKING UP THE ENCAMPMENT AT NIGHT	30
ARTILLERY CROSSING THE NULLAH	45
PLAN OF THE BATTLE OF THE KALA NUDDEE BEFORE THE ADVANCE	70
WHEN THE THIRD SHOT BLEW UP THE TUMBRIL WE GAVE A CHEER, ETC.	72
BHEESTIE PATCHOOLIE	96
SKETCH OF THE POSITION OF THE FORCES AT THE COMMENCEMENT OF THE ACTION OF SHUMSHABAD	102
A MUSSHACH	112
A PIG HUNT	117
MY ESTABLISHMENT	123
NAVAL BRIGADE RACES	128
IN THE SKIRMISH I GOT A SABRE CUT ON MY RIGHT HAND FROM A SEPOY WHOSE THICK SKULL I HAD JUST LAID OPEN	140
SIR WILLIAM PEEL BRINGING HIS GUNS UP IN FRONT OF THE DILKOOSHAH	155
CHANGING HORSES ON THE GRAND TRUNK ROAD	204

RECOLLECTIONS

OF

A WINTER CAMPAIGN IN INDIA.

CHAPTER I.

VOYAGE OUT—ARRIVAL AT ALEXANDRIA—RAILWAY FROM CAIRO ACROSS THE DESERT—SUEZ—CALCUTTA.

WHEN the news of the Indian mutinies reached England, and it was determined to send troops, and some ships there, I applied for employment either to carry troops or in any other way, but without success. Soon afterwards, as each succeeding mail brought accounts of disaster upon disaster, and massacre upon massacre, it flashed upon me that, even if I could not get an appointment, I might, as it is elegantly termed, "go on my own hook," and that one English heart and arm devoted to the good cause, though only like one drop of water in the ocean, would not be without its use. I therefore went up to the Admiralty, got leave for a year to travel in India, and was fortunate in obtaining a passage in an early steamer, and sailed from Southampton, on the 4th of October, in the Peninsular and Oriental steamship, the *Colombo*, Captain Field, master, &c. &c.

We had pleasant weather till we nearly reached Finisterre, when a S.W. gale met us, and we were obliged to lay-to, the wind and sea being too much for the go-ahead qualities of the " good ship *Colombo*."

The captain thought she made good weather of it, I did not; for she shipped some heavy seas, one of which nearly swamped the engine-room; another washed all the people away from the wheel, throwing one man over it, and hurting him severely, besides washing the binnacles, compasses, and everything else that was abaft into the lee scuppers.

However, though I did not think much of the qualities of the *Colombo* as a sea-boat, I did very much admire those of her captain as a seaman; prompt and energetic to remedy anything that went wrong; always on the spot directing and controlling every evolution, by his coolness and firmness he gave confidence to those who, seeing the heaped-up waves in foam-crowned masses, each succeeding one of which more than its predecessor seemed, with the increasing

"SHE SHIPPED SOME HEAVY SEAS"

gale, ready to dash its mountain of water upon the whole length of the struggling ship, would have thought themselves in deadly peril, but that they saw that each time in obedience to a motion of his hand the helmsmen brought the bows of the ship slightly up to the sea, and that she rose, though with difficulty, to it, and then the wave, breaking obliquely along her side, was lost roaring and foaming under her quarter, and struggling and rushing away to leeward.

For the greater part of three days, during which the storm lasted, he remained on deck, constantly watching every motion of the ship, and controlling her. At last the weather moderated, and our head was put the right way, and we proceeded on our voyage rejoicing. There were two very fine horses on board, both of which died in the gale, though everything that under the circumstances could be done to save them was done.

I was equally pleased with Captain Field's knowledge of navigation as with his seamanship, and I learned many things from him; especially the way in which he made new tables of deviation for his compasses, when replaced after being washed away in the gale; and so correct were they, that every landfall which he made going to Gibraltar, Malta, and Alexandria was right to a mile and to half a point of the compass.

We arrived off Alexandria on the evening of Sunday, the 18th, and went into the harbour on Monday morning, and anchored about seven. The Peninsular and Oriental Company's agent came on board, and gave us the news of the capture of Delhi, which was received with three times three. No sooner was the anchor down, than such a jabbering began; about a hundred Arabs were on board in a jiffy, and commenced unlading baggage, and as they make a kind of sing-song noise as they pass it from one to the other, the Babel-like deafening which ensues may be imagined. However, with all their noise, they seemed to have some system, for the traps disappeared with marvellous rapidity.

After a parting breakfast on board the *Colombo*, we —that is Mr. William Elliot, of the Bengal Civil Service, now Commissioner at Burdwan, and I— found ourselves transferred to a small boat with a single Arab boatman, who entertained us with a solo to the time of his oars all the way to the shore, except when occasionally another boatman passed near him, when he varied his song with what, to us uninitiated, appeared unmitigated abuse, but which was, I believe, only a way they have of saying—" How d'ye do, old fellow?"

After a mile's pull, we landed at the wharf near the railroad-station, in the midst of a crowd of passengers —porters with luggage, Arabs screaming and fighting to carry parcels, and almost pulling them out of one's hands; venders of fruit, venders of veils, of matches, of cigars (precious bad ones), solar topes, alias pith hats; hundreds of donkey-boys, all squalling and crying out, "Very good donkey, sar; take 'um to Bumphis Belly, Pattles Sneeres," *i.e.*, Pompey's Pillar and Cleopatra's Needle;—and so, in the midst of this hubbub and noise, we go on pushing, fighting, hustling, and sweating, till we reach the office, where round a single hole are collected half a hundred anxious, and not over civil passengers, shoving and squeezing to get to said hole to obtain their railroad tickets. W. Elliot and I, being both peacefully inclined, waited at the outside of the mob till the crush had subsided, and when we obtained our tickets, found, to all appearance, that the train was full, and rather despaired of getting seats; but on appealing to one of the officials, he discovered in a carriage six passengers and *two dummies*.

The good folks, thinking that the room of any more passengers was better than their company, had heaped upon the two spare seats a lot of cloaks and coats, on the top of each bundle of which a bonnet and veil was placed, and the draperies so artfully disposed as to have the appearance of real passengers of rather retiring dispositions. However, they had to pull down their cleverly-constructed simulations, and we, real flesh and blood, triumphantly took possession of the vacated seats.

Soon afterwards we started, and went along about twenty miles an hour, through a country which appeared one extensive swamp, with occasional topes of date-trees, and collections of what, from their size and shape, might be beavers' huts, but which are the villages of the miserable inhabitants. The height of the roofs is not more than six feet, and the door, or rather entrance-hole, about three, so that they bob in and out more like rabbits in their burrows than creatures rejoicing in the " stature and dignity of" *Man*. After going on about two hours and a-half, we came to the Nile, which we crossed on a floating-bridge, on to which the railroad carriages are pushed—(Said Pacha the other day was pushed a little too far, and the carriage in which he was rolled over into the river, and he was drowned),—and when it reaches the opposite side they are pushed on shore.

This is only a temporary expedient, for they are building a magnificent bridge across. On arriving on the opposite side, we found we were to stay some time for luncheon, which was laid in a wooden pavilion, and was very plentifully supplied; though the viands were not pleasant to look at, yet hunger and a *double apprenticeship* in a midshipman's berth are facts which teach a man to "take things as they come," and I made a capital meal, though I heard plenty of grunting and grumbling all around me. About five we arrived at Cairo, when again began a mighty rush among the passengers to the inn, for it was thought that there would not be beds for all. W. Elliot and I jumped into a carriage and pair, and away we went, forty miles an hour, for Shepherd's Hotel.

We were soon there among twenty others, but found no one of any kind to give an answer to our anxious inquiries for rooms, and the passengers began to arrive in shoals, or *schools*, as Jack calls them; by-and-bye some one told us to go up-stairs, where we found an Arab servant, and of course every one holload at him for accommodation. He immediately rushed about, and, to our surprise, locked all the doors of the rooms, except when some adventurous *party* bolted before him into a room and bagged the key: then some fellow laid hold of him by the arm to force his attention, off he bolted and locked a door; then some strong-minded lady besieged him for room for *self and babby;* away he bolted and locked another door; and had his feet and hands been multiplied, instead of being confined to a pair of each, no doubt all the doors would have been locked, and not even the aforesaid adventurous parties would have got in. It appears that the proprietor, at least so we heard, had promised a dozen of his bedrooms to some passengers who had spoken to him on the subject on board the steamer, and he had sent word to keep them till he came. My chum and I got tired of this door locking, and went to the Hotel d'Orient, where we soon got two nice clean rooms opening into each other, and were instantly with our heads in our basins getting rid of the dust and dirt of an Egyptian journey.

It was too late to see much of Cairo that evening, but we strolled into the bazaar before dinner, and after that went to the gardens of the great square, and enjoyed our pipes and coffee under the trees, a very fair band playing "Rule Britannia," "Ye Gentlemen of England," and many other popular airs for our especial benefit. By-and-bye the spirit of song moved some of our party, and, as Englishmen usually do, they began to roar out that "they wouldn't go home till morning—'till daylight does appear," &c., a proceeding highly edifying to the good people of Cairo, except that, I suppose, they are by this time accustomed to the absurdities and eccentricities of that most self-sufficient monster, John Bull, who, wherever he is, always seems to think, with "Rob Roy," "Mr. Briggs," &c., "that his foot is on his native heath, and his name's MacGregor."

When we came back to the inn we found an *affiche* stuck up, informing us that the train would start at eight the next morning. So, after a night of great luxury, under mosquito curtains, with open windows, we got up early, had a delicious bath, a rambly-scrambly breakfast, and paying the bill, which required almost as much pushing and squeezing to get to the bureau as it did to get the railroad tickets at Alexandria, we strolled to the station, and took our seats. Soon afterwards we were informed that the train would not start till *half-past one*, by which was meant *an hour and a half*, on account of some delay in the up-train from Suez. So there we sat, according to our different temperaments, some growling, some taking it easy. My employment was in learning from *one to ten* in Hindoostanee, a language in which I was making rapid progress, at the rate of *a word and a half* per day. At last the wished-for whistle was heard, and the train dashed up with some twenty trucks full of Arabs; five minutes afterwards we started, and very soon were in the desert, where the eye has not

One green leaf to rest upon.

Nothing but sand, stones, rocks, with occasionally an Arab encampment, or a string of camels plodding their weary way. After a while we arrived at station No. 1—not a magnificent one like that at Paddington, which has helped to reduce the dividends of the unfortunate shareholders to a miserable one per cent.— but a tank pitched on a scaffolding, and two Arab tents. After giving the engine *a drink* we went on again, and repeated the process every twenty miles. At last we arrived at the terminal station, about twenty-three miles from Suez, and there in a large single tent, so thin as scarcely to give any shade, we found a luncheon laid out, but which at first sight appeared to be nothing but swarms of flies of different sizes and shapes—for literally they were so numerous as entirely to hide the viands upon which they were feasting. Many of the more delicately-stomached folks were dreadfully disgusted and put off their feed; but neither cockroach nor fly can beat an old midshipman; so with lots of others of the more hardened class we set to, and, after brushing off our predecessors, discovered chickens as small as sparrows, and lumps of beef, or camel for what I know, and various other condiments, which, washed down with a glass of capital bitter beer, made a tolerable repast for a desert meal.

After a time they began to prepare the vans which were to take us to Suez. The van is a sort of tilted cart, drawn by two mules as wheelers, and two spicy little horses as leaders; but while they are harnessing, a glance at the encampment may be amusing. On approaching it, about a quarter of a mile before you reach the station, you see all the baggage, goods, cargo, and boxes of specie spread out on the ground, and covering half-an-acre, with hundreds of Arabs and people sorting, arranging, and pulling it about; but though there are things there, so I was told, to the amount of a million sterling (there is 500,000*l*. in specie, and nearly the same amount in jewellery, besides many other things of value in great and small packages,) yet it is all safe, for there has been only one theft since the traffic began; and then, when it was traced to a village, the Pacha destroyed not only the thief, but every one in the village also. Eastern justice, to be sure, which, though not in accordance with our notions of right and wrong, has certainly had the effect of converting the greatest thieves in the world into honest men. Indeed, in the East, they reverse our maxim, " that it is better that ten rascals should escape than that one honest man should suffer," for theirs is, " that it is better that ten innocent men should die than that one rogue should get off."

But to return to the baggage, &c., which is first mentioned, because it is the first thing a traveller looks for, so much of his comfort depending upon seeing certain boxes with O. J. J., or whatever it may be, marked upon them. Taking the railroad as the central line of the encampment looking to Suez, on the right is the refreshment pavilion, surrounded by tents, Crimean huts, and various extemporized edifices of all sorts and sizes; on the left an extensive encampment for all the people who are working on the railroad and in its construction. These parts may be considered a sort of core of the station; beyond are thousands of camels squatted down in circles of about a hundred each, with their heads in and their sterns out, and within the circle their conductors sitting at their heads and smoking their pipes. Each camel has a pack-saddle (the hump sticking up through the middle of which prevents its slewing); to this is fastened on either side a strong rope net, in which are placed the various packages which it has to carry to Suez. These circles of camels stretch away an immense distance, nearly as far as the eye (which by-the-bye is not much above their backs) can reach. Beyond the refreshment tent, a couple of hundred yards, are the vans, standing about without any regard to order, and a little further on the horses and mules belonging to them are picketed in lines to the number of about two hundred. One curious feature of the scene is, that though around the station everything, from flies to men, is teeming with life and activity, yet, but for the railway stretching both ways, with its accompanying lines of telegraph wires and their posts, immediately beyond the outer tent the desert is as much the desert as if no human foot had ever trodden its eternal sands.

Meanwhile the harnessing has been going on, and fifteen vans are ready for the first batch (of which I was not one); after the usual pushing and shoving, the right folks were got into the right carriages, and away they started—if start it can be called where every one of the thirty horses and every one of the thirty mules either stood upright on its hind-legs, or began to pull in the opposite direction from its neighbour, and occasionally treating him to a good kick in the ribs. Each of these vans has not only a coachman who holds the ribbons, but also a groom, who is provided with a whip made of *cowcane*, or rhinoceros hide, with which he belabours the mules and horses most furiously; sometimes he is seen tugging at the leaders' heads till they start; then running by their side, and distributing his favours to all four beasts with the most laudable impartiality; then jumping on the shafts, when the wheelers get more than their proper allowance of kicks and whips. It must not, however, be supposed that the groom has all the whipping to himself; very far from it; the coachman also has a very severe and punishing whip, which he does not fail to use to his—or rather to his team's heart's content. After the first batch were fairly off, we went to look at the camels being laden, and it was curious to hear how they grunted and groaned as the burdens were put upon them; some resisted *à l'outrance*, kicking and biting, and one or two trotted off to the desert; however, they were soon brought back, and the others were reduced to obedience with a few cracks of a good big stick.

After a while we saw harnessing going on, and shortly our vans came *wriggling* up. As all who were left behind had to go in the second batch, it did not take long to collect them, and we were soon off, and after a quarter of an hour's

> Backing and filling,
> And tacking and spilling
> Nautical terms, which I'll bet a guinea are
> Describing a course which is not rectilinear,

we got away in a straggling manner, our fourteen

vans occupying a space about a mile in length by half a mile in breadth, and sometimes *two feet* in depth in the sand. After five hours we arrived at Suez, and found, of course, that all the beds had been secured by the first-comers, so that many of our party had to pig it out the best way they could.

We were nearly as well off for dinner as for beds, for the aforesaid first-comers had rejoiced in capital appetites, and had eaten up everything which was in the hotel. About six of us got the remains of the hind leg of a goat, a bottle of pickles, and some bread, which, with some *Alsopp's Pale*, was not so bad after all. Next day we embarked on board the *Nubia*, Captain Tronson, master, and sailed the next morning, and after a very prosperous passage, touching at Aden, Galle, and Madras, arrived at Calcutta on the 12th November. On board the *Nubia* was a detachment of Royal Engineers, of 200 men and officers, under the command of Colonel Harness and Major Nicholson; there were also many officers hastening to their regiments in India to partake in the toils and the glories of the campaign. Among them, Major Payn, of the 53rd, and Major Hume, of the 38th, and Captain Mansfield, of the 33rd, who was going to join his brother, the chief of Sir Colin's staff, as his aide-de-camp, from all of whom I afterwards received much kindness in the field.

There was some difficulty in getting accommodation, as Calcutta was full, from the number of people who had been driven down from the country; but the proprietor of one of the hotels, who came on board, was known to my friend, W. Elliot, and through his interest I got very well put up, and found Major Hume and I were room-fellows in Brown's very comfortable family hotel, and glad we were to exchange the "crib'd, cabin'd, and confined" space of the *Nubia* for a large and airy apartment, though the air was somewhat muggy, and had more mosquitoes than oxygen in it.

CHAPTER II.

TRAVELLING IN INDIA—ARRIVAL AT BENARES—THE ENCAMPMENT.

THE day after my arrival at Calcutta I delivered many letters of introduction with which I was provided, most of them to influential people in the Government, hoping by their assistance to get a lift up country, a very difficult matter, for all the conveyances had been taken up by Government to forward the troops up to the seat of war, and therefore it was not easy for a private individual to make his way up; but from all, from the Governor-General downwards, I got the same answer—"that every seat was wanted for the conveyance of troops, and that civilians, whom Government was anxious to send up to their stations, could not be forwarded, as everything had to give way to the sending the troops." Lord Canning kindly promised if there was a cessation of the pressure he would send me, but when that would be he could not tell. All this was sufficiently discouraging; but as I had not come to India to halt at Calcutta, I determined to get up some way or other; and by inquiring in every direction I found that there was a dâk company which professed to send one carriage daily as far as Benares, but I was told that the horses belonging to it were so execrably bad that they constantly broke down; and besides, that travelling by oneself was quite out of the question—that one was sure to be killed and eaten, and so forth; also, that not speaking their language, I should not be able to gain any information of any rebels or marauders who might be on the road; notwithstanding all which I rejoiced at the chance, and immediately secured the carriage for the next day, and after seeing my agents, Messrs. Mackillop, Stewart, and Co., and arranging my money matters with them, set to work, and packed up what traps I intended to take with me, which was as limited a quantity as I could possibly do with (for on all sides I heard of the impossibility of getting carriage up country, for any large amount of anything), and left the remainder with my agents, and went to bed better pleased, and with a lighter heart than any night of the week I had been obliged to waste at Calcutta.

Next morning (November 20th) I started off, bag and baggage, and crossing the Ganges to Howrah, which is on the other bank of the river from the so-called city of Palaces, and where is the railroad station, was soon seated in the train. There were detachments of Highlanders and Rifles going by the train that day to Ranee-Gunge, where is the present terminus, and which is the first halting-place of the troops on their way to join the army. How glad I felt to be going with them instead of (as I had done on most days that I was detained at Calcutta) strolling down to the pier to see the detachments cross. As soon as they were all seated, and the baggage stowed, whew-ew went the steam-whistle, and away went we at a very fair pace. At one of the intermediate stations three Hindoo gentlemen got into the carriage, and rich ones, too, I should think, by their fatness (no poor man could afford to get so plump and sleek), and by some valuable jewels which peeped out of their otherwise unassuming apparel. Their ancient and unpolluted descent also was plainly discernible, for, as with the Hidalgos of Spain, their blood was evidently *blue*, for their complexions, instead of the clear though dark brown which the Hindoos usually are, looked as if a wash of indigo had been laid under the copper hue of their skin, making them a dirty neutral tint colour, and giving them a very unpleasant, unwholesome appearance.

Their inquisitiveness was very amusing; they cross-questioned me as to where I was going, what was I going for, why I wore such thick shoes, and on many other points equally pertinent, or rather impertinent, to their interests.

When the train arrived at Rance-Gunge, while the troops were falling-in, I got hold of my luggage, and putting it on the heads of various coolies (why they are called coolies it is difficult to say, except that no amount of heat has any effect upon them), started off to the dâk station, and having given my things to the *baboo* (an *n* at the end would not be misapplied), went to the hotel to get something wherewithal to fortify the inward man. While waiting there, two officers came in, and I inquired of them for a certain Major Snodgrass, for whom I had a coat from the head snip at Calcutta, and one of them turned out to be himself, as Paddy would say. We got into conversation about various matters, and I mentioned the difficulty there was in getting a servant in Calcutta who would go up country, and would do more than take charge of one little finger nail, or some such infinitesimally small part of one's economy, and he told me that the commissariat officer would give me a Madrassee if I made application.

Though it seemed curious that servants should be supplied on demand by the commissariat, like a cask of rum or a piece of beef, yet I jumped at the chance, and went to Captain Lowe and made my application. He told me that there were plenty, but that unfortunately they had all gone away for the night, and as I was starting within a couple of hours he was afraid he could not be able to get hold of one; however, he would try, so after thanking him for his civility I returned to the hotel, where I met an old Black Sea acquaintance, G. Smith, the assistant-surgeon of the *Shannon*, with whom I had a long chat about old times and mutual friends. My carriage was at the door, and I was just going to start, when up comes a little Madras man, and says, " I Captain Jones's servant," and in the space of a minute Hydrabad *Malayapen* (or *Malakoff*, as he soon after was named, for

HYDRABAD
MALAYAPEN
ALIAS MALAKOFF

SYCE MUNNOO

London, Saunders & Otley

shortness,) was installed as my valet, butler, cook, interpreter, &c. &c., and all for the sum of twelve rupees per mensem, out of which he was to feed and clothe himself, besides sending nearly half of it home to his family. Malakoff had to go on the top of the carriage with the luggage, and would have to live there for the next three days and nights, and as the latter were then very severe for India, I said to my friend, "Povero diavolo, he'll die of cold." "Oh," says he, "I have my bedding up here, I'll give you a blanket," and went and fetched a first-rate one, in which Malakoff wrapt up and coiled himself down on the top of the carriage, as snug as "a flea in a blanket," "a bug in a rug," or anything else which is comfortable and warm. I heartily thanked Smith for his kindness then, I thank him again now, and I hope at some future time I may have the opportunity of returning not the blanket, but the good service which he then did me.

Well, at last we were off, and though the horses, the first one or two stages, were tolerable, yet as we progressed they got *worser* and *worser*, till we reached the opposite side of the Sone, when they were *none*, but coolies supplied their place.

As soon as we were clear of the encampments, I loaded my pistols, placed my sword handy, and went to sleep. We occasionally passed detachments in bullock-carts, going up to the army, and about midnight came up with one in which was Major Gloster, of the 38th, for whom I also had a coat, and which he seemed very glad to get. I afterwards became very well acquainted with him, and a good kind fellow he was. I last saw him lying badly wounded in the Dilkooshah, but doing well, and I trust he must now be recovered.

The travelling was usually at the rate of about six miles an hour, though, including stoppages, more than a hundred per day was never made. The only wonder was how we got on so well. Some of the ponies were not much bigger than cats; one or two of the horses (for we occasionally had a horse) were *gone in the loins*—a disease of the spine peculiar, I believe, to India, which weakens the hind quarters so much that the horse can scarcely drag them after him—one of them constantly lay down on the road, and the only way in which he could be got on, was for the coachman and syce, after giving a proper allowance of walloping to make him get up, to push at the wheels,

STARTING THE DAK GARRY.

London, Saunders & Otley

and pull at the shafts. Indeed, the usual way of starting, after the beasts were put in, was for half-a-dozen men to get hold of the wheels and shafts, and force the *crittur* on, after which a proper application of the whip kept him going for a certain distance.

On the 22nd, at Shergotty, I fell in with the detachment of Engineers that we had brought out in the *Nubia*, and the officers very kindly wanted me to keep company with them, as the road was not safe; but I could not make up my mind to go two miles an hour, instead of six, and declined the offer. There was also a party of officers and soldiers going on by horse dâk, and I told my drivers to endeavour to keep with them; but their horses were so much better than mine, that I usually arrived at the station for changing horses just as they were departing, so that I did not get much protection from them. The officer in command very civilly said how sorry he was he could not wait, but that he was anxious to join a detachment which was ahead before it crossed the Sone, and he feared he might be attacked before he reached it—not a pleasant anticipation for a single passenger;—however, about midnight, we came up with the detachment, who were halted in a village on the banks of the Sone, and preparing to cross it.

Here the ponies were exchanged for bullocks, as they draw a carriage better through the deep sand which forms the bed of the river. It was now nearly dry, and was two or three miles across, the river itself not being more than two hundred yards wide. On arriving at the opposite side, I found that the carriage was to be pushed by coolies; all the horses they said had been looted a few days before,—a pleasant prospect, as this part of the road from the Sone to the Kurmassa was supposed to be dangerous, it being where Sir Colin and his staff were nearly caught by the mutineers—and there being an order that "officers travelling by horse dâk were on no account to proceed by themselves, but were to join any detachment which might be going up by bullock-train;" and it was certain that should any unpleasant people appear, all the coolies would bolt off, and of course leave me with *Malakoff* to make the best defence we could.

However, hearing that there was a detachment at Sasseram, I thought it would be best to push on there, and find out from the officer in command what was the present state of the road. We reached there about five in the morning, and leaving the carriages a little off the road, I went up to the camp, and after being passed from a sentry to a corporal, and from a corporal to a serjeant, was taken to Major Cotter's tent, who received me with the greatest civility,—no small thing when one is roused up at five o'clock in the morning—had the goat milked and some tea made, and told me that he had come from Benares two days since, and had met nothing unpleasant on the road, and that it was tolerably safe; upon which I went on, and arrived at Benares on the evening of the 23rd, and put up at a very comfortable inn, "The Star," in the cantonments, about four miles out of the city.

The next morning, at breakfast, a sort of *table d'hôte* one, among other officers was Major English, of the 53rd. He had just returned from a very successful tour in the Ramgur district, during which, with 180 of the 53rd and 150 Sikhs, he had attacked and entirely defeated a body of 800 rebels, near Chuttra, who were strongly posted in an intrenched camp, with four guns; and after beating them well, captured their camp, guns, standards, government treasure, elephants, horses, everything in fact, the rebels only escaping with their lives. Many of them were that evening, and next day, caught by the villagers, and brought in and executed.

I told him in conversation that I did not know how to get on, and he most kindly asked me to join his detachment and march up with them, which I accepted with the greatest pleasure. There was not much time for preparation, for the march was the next night, and there was carriage both for self and traps to get, and unluckily the *head swells* for whom I had letters, and who might have helped me, were away for a day or two, but Mr. Tucker, the Judge, for whom I had an introduction, kindly wrote to the Commissariat officer, (the only means of getting anything, as Government had bought or hired every bullock and hackery that could be got), and in a short time I found myself the temporary possessor of a nigger, two bullocks, and as primitive a cart as is to be seen in the world, and of a shape of the remotest antiquity. These Asiatics never change, but go on from generation to generation, from century to century, from age to age, as their fathers had done before them.

The next thing was to get a horse, but again the same story—Government was buying up every horse for the artillery and cavalry. A gentleman (Mr.

Money) hearing of my difficulty, told me he knew Colonel Beecher, who was employed to purchase horses for Government, and that he might know where to put his hand upon one of the rejected ones, which might suit me till a better could be found, and wrote him a note, but he answered, that all those which were rejected he never saw again, but that he would look out for one for me; also that he had a little Arab which he would part with for five hundred rupees, giving it a very good character. In a very short time the horse, together with his syce and grass-cutter, had changed masters, and a good little beast he was, never sick nor tired; many and many are the marches he has carried me, and through some sharpish skirmishes besides, and hardly ever made a false step or stumble—a rare thing in an Arab, as they are notoriously careless walkers. He was a dark brown little animal, about fourteen hands one inch high, but well and compactly put together, and tolerably good-looking.

At about five in the afternoon of the 25th I betook myself, bag and baggage, to the 53rd encampment, which for the next five months was my home—and a very happy home it was.

CHAPTER III.

BREAK UP ENCAMPMENT—MARCH TO ALLAHABAD—RAIL TO CHEMIE — MARCH TO FUTTEYPORE — CLEAR FUTTEYPORE DISTRICT.

NOVEMBER 26th.—At two in the morning the *reveillée* rang out, and immediately, to my unaccustomed ears, began a noise most Babel-like and extraordinary. Niggers chattering, horses neighing and stamping, camels grunting and gurgling, elephants blowing and trumpeting; some camels and elephants refusing to be loaded, and some straying about the camp, their drivers and mahoots running after them and endeavouring to bring them back and into subjection, and using language, to judge from the tone and pitch of the voices, of not the blandest entreaty; and throughout the whole of this discordant din, a constant accompaniment of tick-uh-tack, tick-uh-tack, tick-uh-tack, was kept up, which was the khlassies, or tent-men rapping the tent-pegs to loosen them previous to striking the tents.

BREAKING UP THE ENCAMPMENT AT NIGHT

Day & Son Lith.rs to The Queen.

London, Saunders & Otley

The scene was very fine and grand, for the soldiers and camp-followers set fire to all the straw and litter; and all the various groups came out, some in strong light, when near the bright flame of the burning straw, others in the chiaro-oscura of darkness visible, when farther from it; and the trumpets sounding, the soldiers, some assembling, some striking tents, and loading elephants with them, and bullocks, hackeries, and camels, with their bedding, officers riding about giving orders, the Artillery harnessing and preparing their guns, the baggage filing off the ground, and lastly, the order to advance—the measured tread of the infantry, the pattering of the horses' feet, the jangling of the harness and accoutrements, and the rumbling of the gun-wheels, form altogether a scene most interesting and exciting.

At three we marched off: the detachment, under the command of Colonel Barker, of the Artillery, consisting of the head-quarters of the 13th, Lord Mark Kerr commanding, Major English's detachment of the 53rd, two companies of the Madras Rifles, under Major Caruthers, and a battery of Royal Artillery, under Major Le Mesurier; also about ninety remount horses.

Our first march was about twenty miles, and we did not reach the encamping ground till about ten in the forenoon. A beautiful tope of mango-trees had been chosen for our halting-place, and when the tents came up and were pitched, we found ourselves as comfortable as princes. The officers, as there was no regular mess, were divided into little parties of three or four, and Major English took me into his, which consisted of himself, Captain Cannon, M.N. 17th, attached as commissariat officer to the detachment, and myself; and as the natives are capital extemporary cooks, and, besides, we had brought some *Europe* preserves, soups, &c., we fared sumptuously every day.

It is impossible for any one to have been received with more kindness and cordiality than I was by the officers of the detachment of the 53rd; their names are Captain Fendall, Lieutenants Helsham, Clarke, Taylor, and Dr. Reid.* Lord Mark Kerr, and the officers of the 13th were very good to me, and Colonel

---

* There is a very good story of one of those officers, who is a native of the Emerald Isle. At a dinner given to the officers of a Peruvian frigate at Calcutta by the 53rd, our friend wishing to do the civil to one of their guests, said to him, " Wull ye be after taking wine with me, *Mr. Purruvian ?*" to which his friend replied in a still more racy Corkonian Milesian brogue, " I'm no more a Purruvian

Barker treated me with that frankness and goodness which make him universally beloved by all who have the good fortune to become known to him.

We continued our march to Allahabad by easy stages, seldom going more than twelve or thirteen miles in the day, excepting the last march, which was twenty-six miles, and arrived there on the 30th November.

At Gopee Gunge, on the route, while strolling through the village, we saw a *chattie*, or earthenware pottery manufacture. No large building full of windows and gas lamps, three stories high, crowded with men, women, and children, but an ugly little old nigger (they are called niggers by every one, notwithstanding the sentimentality expressed about that term by some of our wise legislators in St. Stephen's). This little ugly old nigger, then, was squatted on his hams (no one but a nigger or a baboon could squat that way), with his apparatus, which consisted of a stone disk on a central pivot, and a little bit of

---

than you, *Mr. Irishman*, but I shall be happy to take wine with you." I don't mention names, but any one of the 53rd will know well who I mean, and a right good fellow he is.

smooth wood. In the middle of his disk he dabbed down a lump of clay, and with a handle at the edge gave the disk a very rapid rotatory motion, which it retained for some minutes, and while it was revolving, with his hands and the bit of smooth stick he fashioned the clay within and without, and in a few minutes, except the baking, a first-rate and elegantly-formed chattie, or water-jug, was finished. English threw him a rupee, and whether astonishment or delight predominated in his ugly old phiz it is impossible to say.

We also saw a silversmith at work, whose workshop was quite as primitive as the chattie-maker's; his furnace consisted of a small earthenware saucer, his fuel of a small handful of charcoal, and his blowpipe of a piece of bamboo, and yet in about six minutes he converted a quarter rupee piece into a rather handsome ring, which I have now.

On our last day's march into Allahabad, from a place called Baroud, twenty-six miles from it, just after starting we arrested a spy from the Rajah of Jaunpoor, who was endeavouring to ascertain our force; he was brought into Allahabad, and next day tried and hanged.

As soon as I arrived at Allahabad I paid a visit to my naval fellow-creatures, two hundred and fifty of whom, under Lieut. Wilson, formed part of the garrison. Among them I met three or four shipmates, who had been petty-officers in former ships, with whom I often had interesting conversations, and as I was unofficially among them, they used to tell me their opinions very unreservedly. The Naval Brigade take the guards and other duties of the garrison just the same as the soldiers, and are said to do them very well. There is a good story told about two of them on sentry, current in the camp, though it is not endorsed in the Naval Brigade. One who was on sentry on the main works of the fort by moonlight, looking over the parapet saw another who was sentry on the ravelin, or some outwork. Now, Jack, though he could tell the head from the stern of a ship, and perhaps of a horse, had not passed a competitive examination before his admission into the service, and no doubt his education in fortification and engineering had been sadly neglected, and therefore he was not aware that the outwork was part of the fortification which he was so vigilantly guarding, and seeing a man walking up and down outside of what he considered the fort, and of course his head being full of spies, lurking Sepoys, &c. &c., challenged him. The sentry on the outwork, not imagining that it was he who was the subject of his messmate's anxious inquiries, held his peace, upon which Jack in the fort let drive at Jack on the outwork.

The outwork Jack, a little taken aback by the musket-ball whizzing near his head, sung out—"Hallo! that's your game, is it, my buck? Here's let drive at you, then!" and immediately returned the fire.

On their being relieved and taken to the guardhouse, all that passed between them was, "Well, I'm blowed, Jack, but we are mortal bad shots—we are."

While at Allahabad, where we halted three days, we heard of Windham's actions at Cawnpore, and the disasters attending them; and before we left it, which we did on the 4th December, rumours arrived of the Commander-in-Chief's having relieved Lucknow, and brought off all the women, children, and garrison.

The fort of Allahabad is a strange mixture of ancient and modern fortification; it is situated at the apex of the angle formed by the junction of the Jumna and

Ganges, and is in the form of a triangle, the two ancient sides facing respectively the Jumna and Ganges, and the modern side the base fronting the land. The river sides are immense stone walls, of great height and thickness, with circular bastions at intervals, and machicolated crests, very picturesque, but utterly unfit to resist the battering cannon now used in sieges; the land face has all the modern improvements—low bastions and curtains, ditches, scarps and counterscarps, sloping glacis, and winding covertways. The fort was then but slightly garrisoned, but quite sufficiently so to repel any attack which any amount of Sepoys might make upon it. The enemy were in considerable force on the opposite side of the Ganges, under the Rajah of Jaunpoor, and their outlying pickets were on the river bank, not more than three miles from the bridge of boats, which crossed the Ganges under the guns of the fort. The troops passing up the country were encamped on the plain beyond the glacis of the fort.

On the 4th December, at six in the morning, we struck our camp, and marched to the railroad, and all the men, horses, and baggage being stowed, we started, or rather attempted to start at eight, but the train was so much too heavy for the engine that the wheels *skidded,* and though sand and ashes were constantly poured on the rails yet it stopped every five yards, and at last they were obliged to detach half the train, and take the first half to a straighter part of the rail, and then fetch the other half. The railway from Allahabad to where it joins the main line is along the high road, and therefore in some places is very sinuous, especially at each end of the branch line. It took more than two hours to go the first three miles, and they were obliged to put on a second engine where it joined the main-line by a gradient nearly as steep as the roof of a house, and a double curve as bent as a letter S. Another peculiarity of this railroad was, that, as they burn wood, large blazing sparks constantly flew from the chimney, and sometimes lighting on something combustible in the open trucks, set them on fire. There have been several accidents of that sort, and some very dangerous ones, from the fire nearly catching ammunition, &c. However, since then, they have fitted wire-gratings to the top of the funnels, which prevent the escape of so many sparks, and render accidents much less liable to happen.

We arrived at Chemie, then the terminus (though

to Kharga about eight miles further on, was soon opened), and pitched our camp in a well-sheltered spot, the mango-trees being very large, and their foliage very thick.

We remained at Chemie two days awaiting Colonel Barker's column, which was marching by the road, and which arrived at the junction of the *Puckah* and *Cutchah* roads on the evening of the 5th. Puckah being anything strong, well-built, finished, whereas Cutchah anything unfinished, rough, weakly built. With respect to roads, the Puckah is the grand trunk, or any other Macadamized road, the Cutchah the cross country ones. Each day detachments came up, which were sent on in bullock-trains towards the head-quarter army. On the second day a division of the sailors that I had left behind at Allahabad came up, and went forward. On the 7th, early in the morning, Colonel Kelly, of the 34th, arrived with the head of the convoy which he was bringing of the ladies and people from Lucknow, who were to go by the railroad to Allahabad. The wounded, of whom there were about five hundred in the convoy, were to march down the road. They were in a very miserable state, poor people, and there were only four medical men to look after them (no doubt it was impossible to spare more), so that the "groans of the Britons" were piteous to hear.

The Lucknow folks, as far as one saw them, seemed in very good spirits, and did not look at all starved or in bad condition, but very pleasant and happy, delighted, no doubt, to escape from the confinement and horrors they had been enduring for so many months. May they have years of happiness to reward them for their heroic endurance of so much misery.

Two of the lieutenants of the Naval Brigade, Hay and Salmon, were going down wounded, and managed to smuggle themselves into the train, and were received with cordiality, and made as comfortable as possible by the conductor, a gentleman whose name I never knew, but whose civility and obliging behaviour every one who has travelled by his train must remember with pleasure. Captain Rowley Lambert, R.N., was also going down on his way home, which I was very sorry for, as being a fellow-creature, I had hoped to see much of him. I heard afterwards that he had been very useful, and had distinguished himself much at Windham's battle of Cawnpore.

At three in the afternoon of the 7th we struck our camp, and joining Colonel Barker's columns, marched eight miles, and came to a halt for a few hours, and started at half-past three the next morning, and marched sixteen miles into Futteypore, the scene of one of Havelock's victories.

There I met, and was very happy to renew my acquaintance with, Major Knox Babington, whom I knew many years before at Moulmein. He was very glad to see me, and showed me every attention and hospitality in his power during our stay at Futteypore, where he was commanding the 17th Madras Native Infantry, which regiment was at Moulmein when I was there in her Majesty's ship *Pilot*. On going up to breakfast at their mess, I found that I knew all the old hands, and we mutually congratulated ourselves upon meeting again in so unlikely a place as 600 miles above Calcutta for a Madras regiment and a sailor. I also met there Major Middleton, whose brother is a neighbour in Hertfordshire.

Here we halted till the 11th, when orders reached Colonel Barker that he was to clear the Futteypore district of a body of mutineers who had established themselves upon the banks of the Jumna, and being well provided with boats, passed backwards and forwards across the river, and gave considerable annoyance and hindrance to the military and civil communications of the neighbourhood. Also the revenue had not been paid up in that district, and a magistrate, Mr. Probyn, was to accompany us to do justice upon the delinquents, and to collect the money which, till then, had not been forthcoming.

Mr. Probyn was one of the few who escaped from the massacres on the Ganges. He was preserved by Huddeo Bucksh for three months, and then sent safely away. His residence—which a great part of the time was a cowshed—was by no means a comfortable one, and the insults to which he was subjected were constant and annoying, which make his mercy and want of unnecessary severity in the execution of his duty when he had the power of life and death over his former persecutors, most praiseworthy and commendable.

At two in the afternoon we struck our tents, and leaving the principal part of our luggage in charge of the 17th, marched twelve miles to our encampment, and next morning on to Kargha.

The same evening we started, intending to make a

night march of some eighteen miles, but by some misunderstanding, part of the infantry did not move off the ground till some time after the regiment in advance and the artillery, and unluckily taking the wrong road in the dark, did not form a junction again till ten in the morning, at a distance of only a few miles from Kargha; and thus disconcerted Colonel Barker's well-laid plan of surprising the enemy.

After halting an hour to allow that part of the column which had been wandering all night to rest and breakfast, we resumed our march, and soon afterwards, on the advance guard approaching a village, a fusillade commenced upon some Sepoys that were flying out of it, and a few were shot, and one caught and hanged. This little skirmish lasted an hour; after which we halted, while the magistrate was trying some people, and gaining what information the fear of being presently hanged could get out of them, and, to judge by their volubility, there must have been a good deal. On continuing our march, and approaching Khotah, which was a great nest of Sepoys, the road, which had been a baddish cutchah one, ceased altogether, and we had to march across country, which was very much cut up by nullahs; and we had to ford one river, which, though not deep, yet, from the steepness of its banks, caused considerable delay in getting the artillery across, and consequently we did not arrive before Khotah until an hour before dark. As we approached, we saw some horsemen watching our advance, and then gallop off to the village. On arriving sufficiently near, we advanced, covered by a cloud of skirmishers, but there was no opposition, and we found the place deserted. It is situated very beautifully on a cliff overlooking the Jumna, and on reaching its edge we beheld the inhabitants hurrying across the river, some in large boats, and some swimming. A few shots were fired at them, but they were too far to have much effect. English, with some of his people, dashed down to where they were embarking, a quarter of a mile off, and killed a few, but the greater part escaped.

We saw some firing on the opposite side which belonged to a friendly rajah, but with what result we could not ascertain. The next day the village, which was little better than a hornet's nest, was burnt to the ground; and at two P.M. we started on our return, though taking a different course, so as to visit, and to visit with fire and sword, several other rebel-

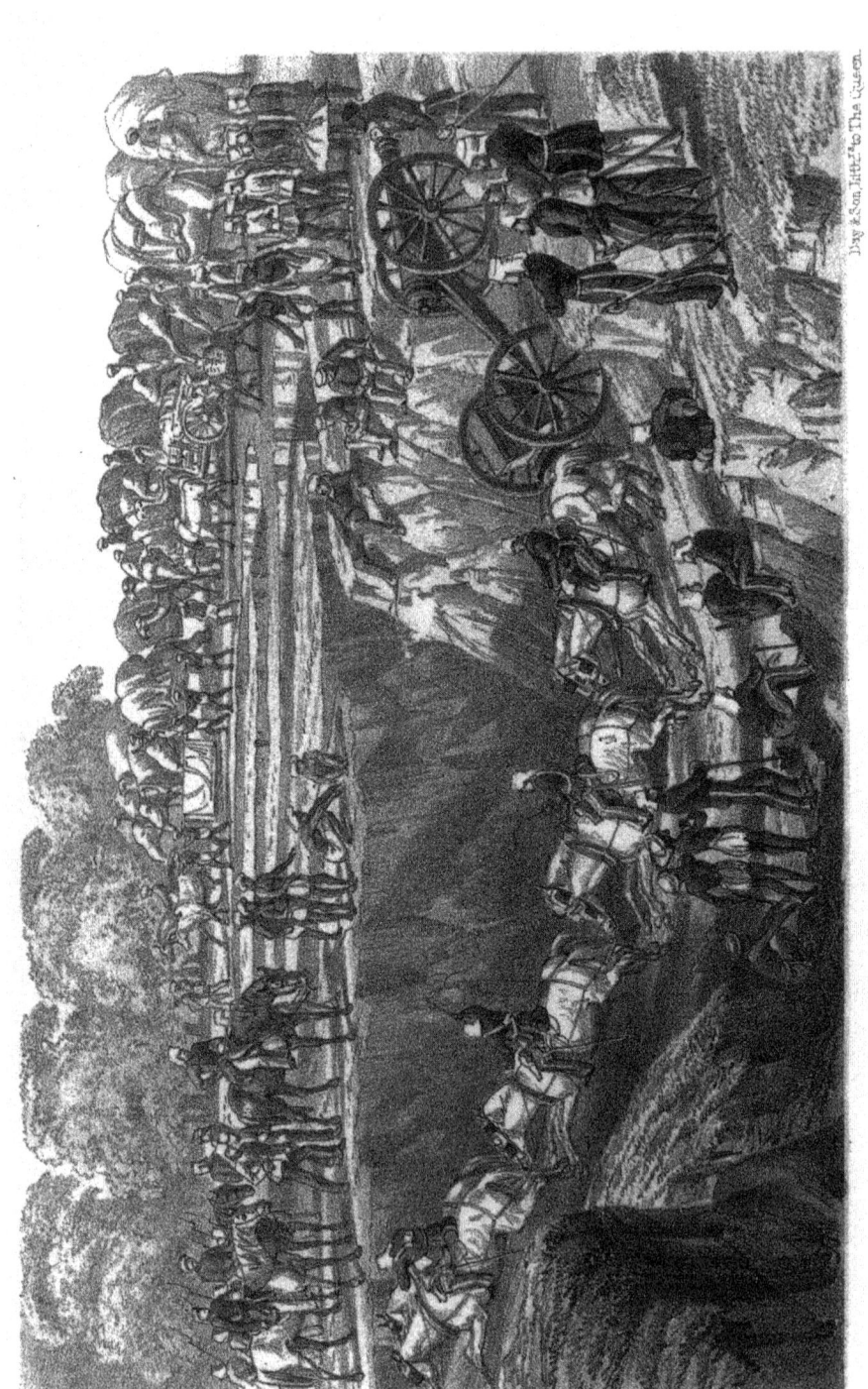

ARTILLERY ROSSING THE NULLAH

lious villages. Just as we were starting, and the greater part of the troops had moved off, my fellow, Malakoff, gave me the pleasant intelligence that my coolies had bolted, but that he had got others, who said they could not or would not carry my things. Now, as my things were absolutely necessary for my comfort, and if I lost them there was no possibility of getting any more, I did what I dare say many philanthropists will blame me for; in fact, I took a big stick and gave the miscreants a good licking all round; after receiving which in very good part, they took up my traps, and carried them to the end of that day's march.

We only proceeded four miles that day, being delayed by a deep nullah, the banks of which had to be broken down, and a road made through it for the artillery.

Next day we continued our march, and burnt a village called Ranek.

On the 16th two detachments were sent to burn two different villages on opposite sides of the line of march. I accompanied the one which went to Lehundah, situated upon the banks of the Jumna. The inhabitants had just time to escape in their boats to the other side of the river. An officer with a few men came up with them just as they were shoving off, and some shots were exchanged.

On returning by a different route I came across a poor wretch with his face half shot off, and his family wailing around him; indeed I was attracted by their cries, and I stayed by them till all the stragglers had passed, to save them from further injury.

Close to, in a cleft in the earth, crouched like hares in their forms, a very old couple were discovered by the soldiers, but who let them alone on my begging them to do so. It is sad work shooting and killing these miserable peasants, while the more active rascals who have committed the atrocities escape, but such is always a servile war, and such its stern necessities.

After burning the village we resumed our march, and rejoined the column.

On the 17th we marched into Futteypore, having passed through a very handsome village, which was spared on account of the youth of the rajah, a boy of nine years old.

CHAPTER IV.

BITHOOR—THE NENA'S PALACE—TREASURE SEEKING—
NAUTICAL ANECDOTE—KANONGE.

THE following morning we resumed our march to Cawnpore. On the road we met a detachment of Artillery and Madras Sepoys, under Brigadier Carthew. Going down under charge were six sailors, who, getting impatient at being left behind at Allahabad, had smuggled themselves into the railroad carriage, and then marched up with a detachment, hoping Sir William Peel would approve of their zeal and let them remain: however, they found him much too good a disciplinarian to allow such a liberty to be taken, and within a few hours of their arrival at head-quarters they were on their way down again. They were looking uncommonly low and down in the mouth as they passed us. We reached Cawnpore on Sunday, 20th, and joined Sir Colin Campbell's encampment, about three miles on the north-west side of it.

That day I made Captain Peel's acquaintance; also delivered some letters to Sir Colin, who received me very kindly, and during the time I continued with his army was always most friendly and cordial.

While we remained at Cawnpore I went tent hunting, a most difficult thing to accomplish, as a very large quantity had been destroyed, and all the tentmakers had dispersed. I at last succeeded in getting a very small one, of the sort called a *pall* (rather an ominous name), about the size of a large dog-kennel; it would just hold my bed and trunks; my chair and table had to stand at the door. However, it was something to have a hole of one's own to creep into.

I also bought a very nice white Arab from Colonel Robertson of the 82nd, who was returning to England.

On the 23rd the camp broke up, the 53rd marching to Bithoor, the rest of the chief's camp moved to an encampment three miles from Bithoor, on the Grand Trunk Road.

It was here where I was first introduced to Sir Hope Grant, whose kindness and friendliness to me, whenever afterwards I had the good fortune to meet him, I have so much reason to rejoice at and be thankful for. The 9th Lancers, of which he was colonel, was a perfect pattern of efficiency and order. After the long campaign they had been through, and the immense quantity of good service they had done, they used to turn out as well-dressed and clean as if they were going to be inspected at Wormwood Scrubs. Every man was dressed in his uniform, and there were no yellow leather boots pulled up over their trousers, and all sorts of motley costume, which obtain in many regiments, and which meets with so much approbation in the present day, but which tends very much to lower the *esprit de corps* and *morale* of regiments. One thing is certain, that with the proper strictness about uniform kept up in the 9th Lancers, there was no happier corps, no corps in which discipline was maintained with less punishment; and one only had to see them in the field to be satisfied that few regiments could equal, none could surpass, the gallant, the dashing, always-to-front 9th Lancers, every man of which, from the colonel to the bugler, looked like a gentleman.

Contrasted with the 9th Lancers in appearance, though equally efficient in their duty, were the squadrons of Punjaubees under Probyn, Watson, and poor

Younghusband. Stern, wiry, dark-looking men, tall and straight of limb, their broad brows overhanging piercing black eyes—their noses rather aquiline and well chiselled—their not too full lips, which, when parted, showed teeth rivalling the whitest ivory, and which were shaded by jet-black mustachios, proudly curled, and their chins covered with silky black beards, carefully parted in the middle, and combed outwards—their voluminously folded blue or red turbans—their grey tunics and bright-coloured vests—their silver-mounted fire-arms, curved scimitars, and lightly-poised lances—the gay caparisons of their well-bitted and often thorough-bred horses—the ease and grace with which they sat and managed them—their proud air and manly bearing, plainly stamped them as belonging to the aristocracy and chivalry of the northern countries of Asia; and on all occasions in this war, well and nobly have they seconded the gallantry and daring courage of their dashing leaders. They are all men of some property, and their horses are their own.

The following day (the 24th) we rode to Bithoor, which was being laid in ruins, at least all the part which belonged to the Nena. His palace was laid low, his mosque blown up, and so completely, that there was literally not one stone left upon another.

There were three wells in his formerly beautiful garden, down which he has thrown a great part of his treasure.

A large working party were busy bailing the water out, and recovering the treasure; a large quantity of gold and silver vessels having been got up.

It was a very difficult operation, for the water stood at 30 feet depth, its surface being 20 or 25 feet below the mouth of the well; and all that water had to be drawn out before the people could work at the bottom; nor could they, with all their exertions, reduce it more than within two feet of the bottom. They had four buckets, of bullock's hides, each holding eight or ten pails full, constantly at work, with about forty men upon each pulley. At night, when the work was performed by bullocks, the water gained upon them to about 13 feet deep, and it took from daylight until eleven or twelve o'clock before the level of the water was sufficiently reduced to work at the bottom. Very large quantities of treasure were recovered after we left. Brigadier Adrian Hope was in command of the magnificent brigade before Bithoor, consisting of the

53rd, 42nd, and 93rd, and some artillery and cavalry. I then had the pleasure of making his acquaintance, which I had many opportunities of improving afterwards. No praise of mine can add to the admiration for his worth or the regret for his loss which have been so feelingly depicted in the Commander-in-Chief's dispatches, and expressed in the letters of his private friends and companions in arms, but I cannot refrain from adding to theirs my humble tribute to the memory of this good and gallant soldier. Daring, though cool in action; firm, but conciliatory in the camp; friendly and cordial in his mess and with his acquaintances, there is but one feeling at his early death, and that is deep, deep regret.

On Christmas-day, Major Payn, who was one of my fellow-passengers, and who warmly greeted me on joining the 53rd mess at Bithoor, received the news of his promotion to the majority in the regiment, at which there was great rejoicing, as he is a great, and deservedly so, an universal favourite in the regiment.

On the 26th, finding that the brigade was likely to remain some days at Bithoor treasure hunting, and that the chief had moved on, I packed up my traps and set out for his camp, which was at a place called

Hoorah, about twelve miles from the former encampment, and arriving there at about half-past nine at night, pitched my tent under a large tree.

Next morning, as soon as the army had got into its line of march, I asked Peel to let me pitch my tent in his camp until my 53rd friends rejoined, which he allowed me to do with great pleasure. The next day the army marched on, but a detachment, under General Windham, was sent to the southward of the road to destroy a fort called Tutteyghur, belonging to a contumacious rajah, and with which I went. About four miles from the road we came to a small river, which it took some time to cross, for the gun-bullocks got unruly in the water, and every one began pulling different ways. Of all the stupid animals in existence, there is none more so than a bullock when it gets into a difficulty; it is as obstinate as a mule, and as stupid as an ass.

While the guns and ammunition were being got over, a magistrate, Mr. Power, was trying some of the people in a village close by. It appeared that an Indigo planter, who lived in the neighbourhood, had been murdered, his factory *looted*, and his property destroyed. Some scoundrel, who fortunately for the ends of justice is generally to be found, turned queen's evidence, and the people were arraigned. An old patriarchal-looking man, with a beard white as snow, was hung (some of the planter's goods were found in his house), and another old man was shot.

Soon afterwards, the guns being got over the river, the corps continued its march, while the Irregular Cavalry scoured the country.

Every now and then they brought in some fellows they had caught with arms in their hands, and occasionally the report of a musket told their fate.

On arriving off the fort, we found the rajah and his people had decamped; he had got information of the chief's kind intentions to him that morning; but though the bird was flown, the nest was still warm.

It was a strongish place, with an outer wall, with circular bastions, which was separated from the inner wall of the fort by a deep ditch.

There were no guns left, for the rajah had taken them and his treasure away.

The place was ordered to be destroyed; and while the engineers were surveying it, a good many people, myself among the number, wandered about the rooms.

In one of them I found a couple of glass candlesticks, not worth sixpence a-piece; but as my establishment only sported an empty porter bottle, I thought they would make a handsome addition, and took them. Coming down stairs I met Forster—poor fellow! he is now dead—one of the Chief's aide-de-camps, who said—"By Jove, old fellow, you'd better not let Sir Colin catch you looting—here he comes!" Upon which I dropped them, as Paddy says, like a hot murphy; and in a couple of minutes after saw a Sikh walking off with my elegant candlesticks. Soon afterwards I saw the Chief serving out *bamboo backsheesh* to some Sikhs who passed him with loot, with a big stick, and I rejoiced at the warning my friend Forster had given me, else, perhaps, in his wrath, he might have broke my head too.

Windham was left with his force, and Sir Colin and his staff, with a slender escort, took a cross country gallop to the new encampment, where the army had moved to during our *détour*.

I found my tent pitched in the Naval Brigade encampment, and dined with Peel; and this was the commencement of a friendship that I shall always remember with satisfaction and pleasure. We had a long chat about naval matters, and of the doings of the Naval Brigade.

One story he told me struck me as very comical, rather in the Marryat style. "An admiral, who commanded on the West India and North American station, not a quarter of a century ago, was very scientific, and his science sometimes became rather a bore. The ship was on her way from Bermuda to Halifax, and there was a difference of opinion between the captain and himself whether they were in the Gulf Stream or not, the Admiral thinking, from the quantity of seaweed floating about, that they were. A sure test is that the temperature of the water in the Gulf Stream is hotter than that of the atmosphere; in every other situation it is colder.

"'Mr. So-and-So,' to the midshipman of the watch, 'bear a hand, and get a bucket of water drawn, and send down to Mr. Diachylon, the assistant-surgeon, for the loan of his thermometer,' says the captain.

"Away skuttles the mid forward to the forecastle. 'Here, you Tom Bowlin,' to the captain of the forecastle, 'draw a bucket of water, sharp! The Admiral wants to know whether we are in the Gulf Stream;' and looking down the fore-scuttle, '*You, Mr. Ship's Cook, just hand a pannikin of boiling water up here out of the coppers,*' which, being added to the bucket of water, was taken aft to the great men. The thermometer was applied, the temperature of the mixture was considerably higher than the atmosphere—the ship was in the Gulf Stream—the Admiral was right, and triumphantly looked, 'I told you so,' to the crestfallen captain. So much for middies' respect for persons; even mighty Admirals are not safe from their pranks in these degenerate days."

Next day we rode to Kanooge, which is said to be one of the oldest cities in India. A lot of mids accompanied us, for, though particular upon duty, Peel liked to see his people happy around him, and was always glad to have his young folks about him whenever he went to any place of interest.

The remains that are still inhabited of the city are not considerable, but the whole country for miles is one mass of brickwork, generally covered with a slight quantity of soil, but very frequently the old walls crop out. There are some handsome mosques and tombs in what is called the *modern* town; they are coeval with the first introduction of Mahometanism into India.

Here Sir Hope Grant had a successful engagement with a large body of the mutineers, and drove them, in the pursuit, towards the river, the Kala Nuddee. A party, who were hotly pursued, were all destroyed but one man, whose escape was rather curious. He had got a little way in the river, when the troopers, who dashed up, called him back, which, as, I suppose, he concluded that his hour was come, he obeyed. One of the men snapped a pistol at his head, but it missed fire, upon which he changed his mind, and thinking, probably, that he had been premature in his former conclusion about his fate, made a bolt for it, and swam across the river under a shower of bullets, and escaped.

However, some two or three hundred bit the dust, so that one escape was of no great consequence.

CHAPTER V.

THE NAVAL BRIGADE—BATTLE OF KALA NUDDEE—FUTTYGHUR—THE ENFIELD RIFLE.

I REMAINED for some days in the Naval Brigade camp, until my 53rd friends rejoined the head-quarters. I was much pleased with the excellent order and discipline which was maintained, and the cleanliness and neatness which prevailed. The men in particular were as well dressed and as clean as they would have been on board the *Shannon* herself, or any other man-of-war in good order.

On parade they moved with the precision of a well-drilled corps, and they handled their arms as men who knew how to use them; and to see them "march past" or advance in line, would have done a soldier's heart good.

It appeared wonderful to me how sailors could be trained to be so steady; and the manner in which they worked their heavy guns was the admiration of every one, from the Commander-in-Chief downwards. In fact, the brigade was a credit to Captain Peel, his officers, and every man in it.

The number of pets which the sailors had was marvellous—monkeys, parrots, pigs, guinea-pigs, dogs, cats, mon*gooses* or mon*geese*, which you like, and lots of other creatures. Some of the monkeys were as tame and affectionate, and would follow their masters like dogs. Peel often said "the *Shannon* would be a regular menagerie when they got back to her."

Their big guns were drawn by thirteen pair of oxen, or by a couple of elephants. Along well-made roads, on good ground, where there are no nullahs to cross or obstacles to get over, the bullocks are much preferred; they go on steadily at a certain rate, about two and a half miles an hour, for from twelve to sixteen miles per day for weeks together, without knocking up, and give very little trouble; but if the gun has to cross rivers, sands, nullahs, or broken ground, they are the stupidest beasts in the world, pull different ways, or pull not at all, get their heads clear of their yokes, kick, butt, and give all manner of trouble, which, with the cries, beating, kicking, and *tail-twisting*, inflicted upon them by their drivers, creates a Babel-like noise and confusion seldom to be enjoyed out of India. Meanwhile the gun sticks fast, and probably is sinking deeper and deeper in the sand or mud, or whatever it may be, till at last an elephant is brought up, who goes behind it and gives it a push or shove in the cleverest way; and when the strain is lightened, the bullocks are induced to renew their efforts; or, a couple of hundred men clap on the drag-ropes, and pull it out by main strength. The elephants, how clever soever they are in getting the guns over bad and broken ground, have one great fault. In their *wisdom* they dislike extremely going under fire, and if they are hit, become unmanageable, and bolt off anywhere, to the great danger and discomfort of those in their way, besides the loss of the use of the gun for some time; whereas the bullock will advance under the heaviest volleys of musketry and cannon with the utmost unconcern; and even if they are hit, take it in the most praiseworthy and philosophical manner.

There are no ammunition-boxes upon their limbers, as on those of field-ordnance—the gun being considered sufficiently heavy without any additional weight—but an ammunition-wagon, drawn by six bullocks, is attached and follows close to each gun, for immediate service, besides dozens of them belonging to the battery generally.

I may here mention my opinion, that the system so successfully introduced by Sir William Peel of bringing the heavy guns to the front, even up with the skirmishers, has this risk, that how formidable and useful soever they are, as long as the fight is an advancing or winning one, yet, should there be a check, or the skirmishers be driven in, the guns would probably be lost, as the limbering-up and harnessing the bullocks to them is a longish job; nor could they retreat as fast as men could march quickly to the rear.

When the 24-pounders were put in Peel's hands, they were not fitted with sights; but he immediately had some made, the best I have ever seen. A dispart was fixed on the muzzle of the gun, with a notch along it; the tangent sight was a long screw fitted into a hole bored through the cascable, pointed at the top, with a cross-arm to turn it round, by which means the elevation was adjusted.

Its advantages were, that there was the whole length of the gun between the sights, which made an error of pointing twice as easily corrected as if the dispart had been where it is usually placed, at about half the length of the gun, and the elevation could be, by the slightest turn of the screw, adjusted to the minutest part of a degree; and the result was, as Captain Peel observed, "It should not be said of these guns that one can shoot with them as well as with a rifle, but rather that one can shoot with a rifle as well as with them."

I was much surprised at the heavy field-guns in India not being sighted, and asked a distinguished officer in the Bengal Artillery how it was? He said he did not think it of any consequence—that they got the range with one or two shots, and this did very well! The Royal Artillery, however, fitted all the guns which came into their charge with sights. I do not know whether the Bengal Artillery thought better of their rough-and-ready plan or not.

We remained at our present encampment till the 31st December, when Windham's force having rejoined head-quarters, we marched to Goordah Gunge, where the Furrikabad road branches off from the Grand Trunk road; here we heard that the rebels had burned the bridge over the Kala Nuddee.

The line of march was formed on the road just before

daybreak. All the baggage animals, wagons, camp followers, led horses, &c., being on the right flank, the left being kept quite clear. Soon after the army had moved on, Sir Colin and his staff would be seen cantering along the line, and woe betide any unlucky regiment which was not closed up, or had an interval between its head and the rear of its predecessor.

The usual practice on the march, after the force had proceeded about three miles, was to halt for a short time to allow the rear to close up, the line always lengthening out as it advanced; the arms were piled, the cavalry and artillery dismounted, and the men were allowed to fall out. The Bheasties replenish their mushhuks, and all have a rest. In about twenty minutes the bugles sound for the infantry to fall in, the cavalry and artillery to prepare to mount; the arms are unpiled, the troopers mount, and the word is "Forward." In a march of twelve or fourteen miles there are usually three such halts.

At the last halt, which is much the longest, the Assistant Quartermaster-General and his staff, those belonging to the divisions and brigades, and the Quartermasters of the regiments, with their sergeants, usually move on, if the coast is clear, so as to reach the new encamping ground, and have it marked out in readiness for the arrival of the force.

A convenient spot, often in a fine tope of trees, is selected for the head-quarters camp, which forms a long and broad canvas street, in the centre of which stands the chief's unpresuming tent, marked by the Union Jack floating in the breeze in its front. The divisions of the army are usually on opposite sides of the road, if the encamping ground admits of that arrangement; if not, there is a broadish line between them. Each brigade is separated by a line of demarcation from its neighbours, and each regiment also has its boundary line. The Generals of Division and their staff have their tents in the centre rear of their divisions, and the Brigadiers corresponding positions in their brigades. The regimental camps are divided by roads like a capsized letter T, the stem of which separates the wings, and the cross part forms the officers' quarters, the commanding officer's tent being in the centre, opposite to which, at the end of the road is the quarter-guard, which is slightly in front of the camp. The hospital is in the rear of the officers' quarters, and the baggage animals, bazaar, &c., in rear of all. Each brigade has its distinguishing flag, and so has every regiment, and little flags of the same pattern are stuck into the ground where each tent is to be pitched, and as the same formation is usually preserved, directly one arrives on the ground one knows the site of one's canvas home. Mine was the third on the right of the commanding officer, and I believe my beasts knew it as well as myself, and would have gone to it without any guidance; at any rate, they always seemed to be aware their journey was at an end when they arrived at the little red flag with 53 embroidered on it.

On the arrival of the army at the encamping-ground, the quartermasters are in attendance to pilot the regiments to the places allotted to them; guards are told off, and pickets thrown out, and on the coming up of the baggage, the heads of which soon begin to defile through the camp to their various belongings, the canvas city commences rearing its snowy walls; things are unpacked; bheesties in requisition to pour the refreshing mushhuks over the dried, dusty, and weary thousands; horses are picketed, cleaned, fed, and watered; cooking places built, fires lighted, and condiments got in preparation; camels and elephants, after being unladen, taken off in long strings to browse and water; and in a marvellously short space of time everything has settled down as quietly as if the army had been encamped there a week instead of having just arrived.

The horses are, what nautical men call, "moored head and stern," that is, they are made fast both with head ropes and heel ropes to strong pegs driven firmly in the ground—a necessary precaution, as being generally neither of the feminine nor neuter, but of the masculine gender, they, like almost all male beasts, man included, are given to fight, tear, and destroy each other.

The bullocks generally remain tethered to their carts; the elephants, which are well away from the other beasts, are secured with chains fast to their legs, and to iron pegs; and the camels tied by their nose-strings to each other, or to very slight pegs stuck in the ground. They are nasty fellows to get too near, as they are very apt to bite, and a very severe torn wound they make if they catch hold of one.

The next day, January 1st, 1858, Adrian Hope's brigade, which had rejoined the head-quarters, marched to the Kala Nuddee, taking with them some Royal

Engineers under Major Nicholson, and materials for repairing the bridge, and a division of the Naval Brigade.

It is a suspension bridge with several piers, the road part between two of which was burnt, leaving a vacancy of about thirty or thirty-five feet. Nicholson immediately commenced repairing it, and fortunately several balks of timber were found, which clearly had been felled for the repair of the bridge, or that had been over and above what had been wanted for its construction, lying at the other end. A few planks were soon got across the chasm, and a picket of 100 men posted at the opposite end. They worked hard at the repairs all night, and by eight o'clock the next morning it was sufficiently forward for troops to cross over. Several of us sauntered down to see the night's performance, and I strolled over to see the fellows in the picket, which was furnished by the 53rd. They were saying that during the night a sentry had thought he had heard a bugle, and Flood, of the 53rd, (such a good fellow!) with whom I was chatting, said, "By Jove, I hear it now!" We went a hundred yards to the front to get away from the chattering, and to listen, and sure enough we heard not only the bugles sounding the advance, but the rattle of the wheels of artillery. Flood immediately fell in his picket, and then threw them out in skirmishing order behind some banks and buildings on each side of the road. Fortunately at this moment a working party, with their arms, of the 53rd, crossed, which was much wanted to reinforce the first picket, for the enemy now opened with cannon and musketry, and sent out a swarm of skirmishers, but which were quickly checked by our pickets, and retired to the village in front of us. Sir Colin arrived at this moment with his staff, having ridden over from his camp merely to see how the bridge was getting on, as neither he nor any one else expected any resistance. An aide-de-camp was immediately sent back to order up Greathead's brigade. Major Payn, of the 53rd, crossed over to take command of the advanced posts, and I thought I could not make myself more useful than offering to be his aide-de-camp, which he kindly accepted, and sent me for instructions, so I galloped back to Sir Colin, who sent orders that Payn was to command the advanced posts, and to do his best; and Payn immediately set to work to post his men most advantageously to prevent the advance of the enemy, and to return a heavy fire of musketry which they were keeping up from the village and the topes of trees in our front.

Meanwhile three of the heavy guns of the Naval Brigade had got into action, and were pouring their shot with telling accuracy into the village, and two batteries of artillery were also sending their "winged messengers of death" among the enemy, who replied with vigour from some guns in the village, and from a large gun behind it. Meantime the troops were pouring over the bridge; the staff also, and the cavalry, consisting of the 9th Lancers, and Probyn's and Younghusband's Punjaubees, crossed over, and were posted out of fire behind some buildings until they were wanted. Peel also had come up, and had taken charge of his guns, which had been under the command of Vaughan, the first lieutenant.

Major English overheard, in the early part of the day, a very flattering compliment paid to Vaughan by some of his 53rd. Speaking of the naval guns, one said, "Is *Paal* with us to-day?" "No," said the other. "Who is it then?" "Why, sure it's the chap with the glass in his eye—and he's *nearly as good as the other!*"

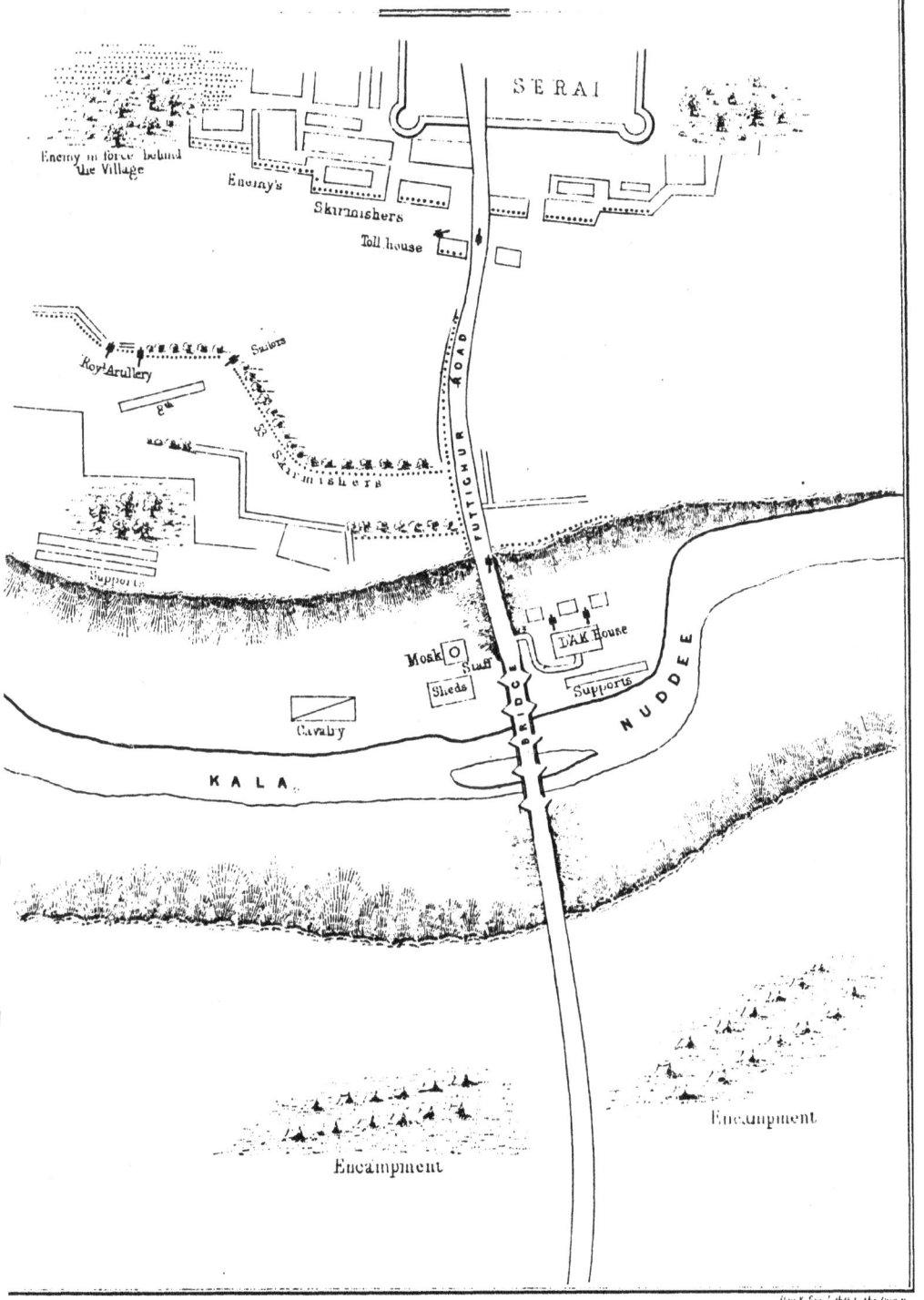

To be classed with Peel was to be placed as high as one well could be.

Vaughan was short-sighted, and always wore an eye-glass.

During this time the bullets were flying about very plentifully, and both Sir Colin and General Grant were struck, though fortunately the bullets were spent, and neither the one nor the other was seriously hurt. About noon Greathead's brigade arrived. There was a gun at the toll-house at the entrance of the village which was doing mischief, and Peel took one of his 24-pounders (they are great iron siege guns of 50 cwt.) up to the front line of skirmishers, and the first shot knocked the gun over, the third blew up the tumbril —practice which is not often equalled; the gun was laid by Vaughan, a capital shot, and as cool when under a shower of bullets as if there were no such thing as gunpowder and lead. It was a good thing to silence that gun, for just before a shot from it killed five and mortally wounded two of the 8th Regiment, which was there in support of the guns. The gun enfiladed them, and a whole section went down dead. They were advanced afterwards a little more under cover, and ordered to lie down, upon which the gun opened grape upon them and us, and though it ploughed up the ground all around, fortunately did not hit any more; notwithstanding that, we were very glad to see its wheels fly up in the air, when struck by Vaughan's well-laid gun, and when the third shot blew up the tumbril, we gave a cheer that might have been heard for miles, and no doubt it had its effect upon the enemy in the village, for their fire sensibly slackened. Shortly before this time poor Captain Maxwell, of the Bengal army, who was attached as interpreter to the Naval Brigade, came up, but before he had been there five minutes a bullet struck him above the knee, and wounded him badly.

My horse was there, so I galloped back for a surgeon, and meeting some of the 53rd officers, told them an officer was wounded in front. Dr. Grant immediately said, "Show me where," and came to the front under a brisk fire, and there, as much exposed as any one, examined and dressed the wound. A noble fellow is Dr. Grant, always ready, whether on the field or in the camp, to succour the wounded or the sick; and I have seen him in an assault as handy with his sword and revolver as with his less chivalric but equally honourable bandages and plaster.

"WHEN THE THIRD SHOT BLEW UP THE TUMBRIL WE GAVE A CHEER" &c.

London, Saunders & Otley

When going for the doctor, squatting behind a tree, close to the front of the skirmishers, I saw my worthy factotum, Malakoff, who had brought some wine and biscuits, and a box of grapes, (which we used to procure from Afghans who yearly make a pilgrimage into Hindostan to sell the delicious produce of their more favoured country). Some of the native servants are very bold, and do not mind exposing themselves to fire, or to any danger to serve their masters; the Syces and Bheesties in particular are always with their masters or the regiments to which they belong.

I took the grapes to Maxwell, and when he had taken what he wanted, shared the remainder with Peel's aides-de-camp, two fine little mids about fifteen years old (Lascelles and Watson by name), who used to stick to him like his shadow, under whatever fire he went, and seemed perfectly indifferent to the whizzing of bullets or the plunging of cannon-balls.

Soon afterwards, as the fire had almost ceased, some of us assembled round the 53rd mess-dhoolie, and discussed some luncheon and pale ale. While the inward man is being refreshed, I will relate an anecdote which, though well-known and laughed at in India, is not so widely spread at home. One of our great

Parliament men, no matter whom, in describing one of the battles of the Suttlege campaign, to add to the horrors of his description, said that "on the advance of our troops, hundreds of *ferocious* dhoolies rushed down the hill, and in a few minutes the plain was swept of the wretched wounded." He was not perhaps aware that a dhoolie is a hospital litter for conveying the wounded, and in some instances is diverted from its proper use to that of carrying the mess grub.

While we were employed in the above unwarlike manner, the 53rd skirmishers arose suddenly with a shout, and made a rush for the village. "By Jove," exclaims Major English, "what will Sir Colin say? MacNeil (to the adjutant), for heaven's sake go and stop them." "My horse is here, shall I go, too, English?" "Do; that's a good fellow;" and away we went at a gallop, and reached the village just with the foremost men. It was fortunate for us that the enemy did not wait for the gallant 53rd, or two horsemen nearly in front would have had not much chance. MacNeil was halting them, while the advance sounded, and hurrah! on they went. The advance was first sounded by a little drummer-boy of the 53rd (so we heard afterwards) who stuck himself up on a mound and too-tooed away the advance and the double with all the breath in his lungs. When asked afterwards what he meant by sounding it without orders, he said, "Please, sir, I was afraid the men would lick me if I didn't." The first thing we met was the gun Peel, or rather Vaughan, had knocked over, with the gunner lying dead by it.

Payn now came up, and taking command, got the men into order, and advanced through the village, and on clearing it, opened them out in skirmishing order, still advancing rapidly. We could only see the stragglers till we crested the hill, a short way in rear of the village, and then beheld the enemy drawn up about half a mile from us, with their artillery in front of them, which immediately opened a sharp but ineffectual fire.

On looking to our left we beheld with joy our cavalry advancing at a gallop, threatening the enemy's right, and behind us our artillery coming up rapidly, and the infantry advancing beyond the village; so the 53rd kept pressing on. The artillery soon opened upon the enemy, and as the cavalry were now getting close to them, they broke and dispersed like a fan all over the country. In a moment the cavalry were among them, and soon about 300 were cut up, the remainder saving themselves by flight, and by the mysterious manner in which an Indian force disappears. One moment the ground is covered in every direction with fugitives, the next there is hardly one to be seen; they hide in the long grass, in the cutes of dholl, which grow six feet high, in the cracks and clefts of the earth, in holes, in ditches, behind walls, behind banks, behind everything or anything which can conceal a man. Occasionally they are discovered, and their fate is soon sealed, but the greater part escape.

We captured seven guns out of nine which they had, and as the furthest was at the tenth milestone from Futtyghur, and the Kala Nuddee at the 17th, Sir Colin may, in great part, thank the dashing but rather irregular advance of the 53rd for his success on that day, for had the advance been much longer delayed, the greater part would have got back in safety to Futtyghur and Furrukabad, and instead of having merely to take possession of an empty fort, he might have had to besiege it, thereby wasting much valuable time and many equally valuable lives.

On inquiry, it appeared that it was whispered

amongst the 53rd, that the 93rd, who were ordered to dine early on purpose, were to be sent on to storm the village, and they, thinking it very hard that after being under fire for seven hours, they should be cut out of the honour of storming the place, passed the word to one another to advance while the 93rd were dining. Afterwards, when Sir Colin came up with some of them (I will not answer for the truth of this, but I have been told it a hundred times, though I have also heard it denied), and began pitching into them for daring to advance without orders, all the reply he got was "Three cheers for Sir Colin;" and on his turning to Mansfield, and saying—"Speak to them, they are your old regiment," there was immediately "Three cheers for General Mansfield." Meanwhile an order was given for a general advance, and the baggage was directed to cross the bridge, and to come on; I cantered on to the front to see what had been done there, and when about a mile on I met an artillery officer who said "You had better not go on; there are several desperate fellows in a hole there who have killed and wounded some men, and they are holding some of the Naval Brigade at bay." Not quite seeing his argument, I galloped on rather faster, for two reasons: first, to get there sooner, and secondly, that if they did take a shot at me it should be a flying one; and came up to Peel, who had with him young Daniels and half-a-dozen men; (Daniels is the mid who was Peel's aide-de-camp during the Crimean war, was at his side during the slaughter of Inkermann, and bound up his wound at the repulse of the 18th of June, under the storm of shot, shell, and bullets which the Redan was pouring into our shattered forces, and helped him back to the trenches; he has the Victoria Cross, and medals without end, and is a fine fellow indeed). They were standing behind some trees. Peel said "Get off your horse or you'll be shot," which I did sharp. Alongside the road was a ditch, about six feet deep, in which were four Sepoys, two dead; young Daniels had shot one with his revolver, the two others at that moment jumped up and bolted into a little house by the roadside, which had been a police-station. I took my pistol from my holster (I had left my sword hanging to the mess-dhoolie when I started off in such a hurry), and running up to the window, looked out for a chance to get a shot at them, but could only see the points of their bayonets sticking out of the inner doors; one poked his head out for a moment, and I snapped a shot, but missed him, and I saw the muzzle of his musket nearly point at me; it could not luckily quite do so, for the corners of the door did not allow enough training. A shot came from another direction, which I suppose killed one, and the other made a rush; and I did not miss him this time, but rolled him over dead—my first subscription to the punishment of the murderers of our countrymen, our countrywomen, and their helpless children. I rejoiced at it, and felt that now I had not come out to India in vain. Soon after a dhoolie passed, and on inquiring whom it contained, we were told it was poor Captain Younghusband. He had been through the siege of Delhi, hadl ed his gallant Punjaubees in all the fights in Greathead's and Grant's descent from Delhi to Cawnpore, had had the most marvellous escape shortly before, for in a pursuit he and his horse fell down a well, and two more came on top of him, yet, wonderful to relate, he was got out unhurt, the others, horses and men, were killed; and here, in cutting up these fugitives, he, as fate would have it, came across one determined man among many cowards, who, knowing his own death inevitable, knelt down on one knee, took a deliberate aim when Younghusband was within five yards of him, shot him through the lungs, and was himself immediately killed. Younghusband lingered on till next day, when he expired.

Captain Probyn led his troop most gallantly that day, as he did on all occasions; there never was a better leader of irregular troops; tall, handsome, a fearless rider, a splendid swordsman, kind in disposition, affable in manner, he was adored by his men, and admired by all who knew him; he would dash into the thickest of the fight, and he and his troop always left a long line of dead marking their headlong career. He enjoyed the affection and esteem of all with whom he served, from Sir Colin Campbell down to the youngest sowar.

Lieutenant Roberts, of the Bengal Artillery, General Grant's Assistant Quartermaster-general, also made himself conspicuous by his gallantry in the cavalry pursuit, and earned the much-coveted decoration of the Victoria Cross. He is one of those rare men who, to uncommon daring and bravery in the field, and unflinching, hard-working discharge of duty in the camp, adds the charms of cheering and unaffected kindness and hospitality in the tent, and his acquaintance and friendship are high prizes to those who obtain them.

Young Anson, too, General Grant's aide-de-camp, distinguished himself particularly. Gentle and quiet in manner—indeed, like Haydee's father, in *Don Juan*,

> The *mildest mannered* man
> That ever waved a sword or cut a throat;

indeed, he seemed to have a peculiar vocation for killing Sepoys; and after a fight his sword was sure to have lost its sheen, and to be dripping with the gore of those who, knowing no mercy themselves, deserved none, and certainly got none during the heat and ardour of battle.

The fight was now over, and it being late in the evening, the advanced troops were recalled to the camp, which had been marked out about three miles from the Kala Nuddee. Our loss was about ten killed and thirty wounded. The enemy's force, from the information which was afterwards obtained, was about 2000 infantry, 500 cavalry, and nine guns.

As the baggage had to defile over the bridge, it was very late before it came up. Mine did not arrive till two in the morning; but I got a heap of straw, and with my tweed plaid over me, I was soon fast asleep, and was rather savage with Malakoff when he woke me to say the tent was pitched and the bed ready.

It is marvellous what fools those who direct the Sepoys and rebels are. If, instead of waiting till we had time to repair the bridge, they had arranged their operations so as to attack us when we first came to it, or rather when it was half completed, when the pickets and working parties on the left bank were isolated, and had no means of communication with the force on the right bank, they would have caused us much delay and perhaps loss; for there was no ford near—at least none for artillery—and it is a very different thing to repair a bridge under a heavy fire, and to do so when unopposed.

If ever people fought when they should not, and did not fight when they should, it is these wretched mutineers.

The next day we marched on to Futtyghur. One of the features peculiar to the advance of the army is the erection of the electric telegraph posts, and the stretching along of the speaking wire. This important operation was in charge of Lieutenant Patrick Stewart, of the Bengal Engineers—a very distinguished and gallant young officer, who stands very high in the estimation of the chief and all who are with him. He was generally a few miles in advance of the army, so that his duty was one of great danger, as well as of the highest utility.

The command which the telegraph gives to Sir Colin over his widely-dispersed forces, and the power of combination which it affords, are incalculable advantages.

As we approached Futtyghur we saw on all sides signs of the destruction caused by the mutiny. Handsome bungalows destroyed, churches pillaged and ransacked, and gardens that had been beautifully kept now overgrown with grass and weeds.

We found the fort evacuated, and in such haste had the Nawab of Furrukabad and his troops bolted, after the thrashing they had got the day before, that they had not destroyed the stores and materials for making the gun-carriages, of which the principal manufactory in India is in the fort of Futtyghur. There were immense quantities of seasoned wood, mostly shaped out in the rough, which could not have been replaced for years, and which a single torch would soon have reduced to ashes.

A detachment was sent into the fort to secure it. A regiment marched down to take possession of the bridge of boats over the Ganges, which had not been injured in the hasty retreat of the rebels, and the rest of the army encamped in the parade ground; a large level piece of ground, with a spacious tank in the middle of it.

For some time the armourers of the 53rd were employed in drawing the bullets out of many of their Enfield rifles, which, in the long firing at the Kala Nuddee, where some men had fired seventy or eighty shots, had got so foul that they could not be loaded. Many bullets had stuck so fast that, after the breech had been taken out, they could not even be forced back through the muzzle, and were obliged to be bored out, and it is evident that long before they got so foul as to be utterly impossible to be loaded, it had become a matter of time and great exertion to force the bullet home. That this is a great disadvantage in the weapon is plain; and in disastrous retreats, like the affairs at Arrah, many men lose their lives, and more, their confidence and discipline, from their utter inability to load their fire-arms quickly when pressed by a pursuing foe.

The quantity of distant popping which goes on, from the belief in the accuracy and long range of the arm, is also very absurd.

In going through the village at the Kala Nuddee that we had been firing at for six or seven hours, expending some thousands of cartridges, I only saw one dead man (there may have been many more that I did not see), and he was killed by a cannon-ball.

The fort of Futtyghur is a large enclosure, surrounded by high and thick mud walls, and a deep ditch, with circular bastions at the angles, and semicircular ones along the faces at regular intervals; the gateway was handsome, and inside it we found an 8-inch howitzer, charged with grape, intended, no doubt, for our peculiar benefit.

The face which looks upon the river Ganges, which flows under its walls, is of considerable height, some fifty or sixty feet, and it was down this that the garrison, or rather its defenders, with the women and children—for garrison there was none—lowered themselves to escape in their boats, but who, all but a Mr. Jones, who was left behind in a village ill, where he was taken care of by the Zemindar, were murdered on their passage down the river by the Nana.

Sir Colin remained encamped here for a month, waiting for the junction of Colonel Seaton's column, and for various combinations which he was carrying out.

The doings and occurrences of which month will form the subject of another chapter.

CHAPTER VI.

AN EXECUTION—FURRUKABAD—INDIAN JUSTICE—RACES— A NIGHT EXPEDITION.

THOUGH we had, through the evacuation and hasty retreat of the Nawab of Furrukabad, obtained possession of the Fort of Futtyghur, and of the old cantonments and the surrounding villages, yet Furrukabad still held out. *Somebody* Khan, who was deeply implicated in the barbarities practised upon our women and children, who were murdered there at the mutiny, upon the retreat of the Nawab proclaimed himself king, and professed his intention of holding out and defending the town.

He had a couple of guns and a few Sepoys, and a mob of Budmashes under his orders; but Sir Colin sent to say, that if he were not given up, he would bombard the town. During the night he was brought as a prisoner into the camp, and all resistance ceased.

The next day Peel and I went to the fort, and while there saw poor Younghusband's funeral. He was buried in the cemetery in the fort.

The mutineers had defaced and broken the greater part of the monuments and grave-stones, but the graves themselves had not been molested or desecrated.

After the funeral was over, we went to Furrukabad to see the execution of the ephemeral king. Poor wretch! he only enjoyed his usurpation for a very few hours.

There is a principal street which runs through the whole length of the town, which is divided by six or seven gateways, some very handsome. Close to the middle one grew a fine tree, and this, from its central position, was chosen for the place of execution, one of the branches of the tree being made use of for the gallows.

We found an immense crowd collected, both of natives and inhabitants, and of the idlers from the camp, besides a considerable military force to maintain order.

One would have thought that, on so serious an occasion as that of an execution, especially of a person of rank, there would have been some decorum and decency of behaviour; but on the contrary, most people seemed to think very lightly of it, and were cutting their gibes and cracking their jokes.

Some country people came up with some poultry, which was seized and sold by a mock auction, by an officer acting as auctioneer; in the middle of which *good fun* the guard with the convict arrived.

He was tied down on a charpoy—a sort of native bedstead—and carried under the fatal tree, upon which he cast an anxious look when he saw the noose suspended therefrom.

He was then stripped, flogged, and hanged. He had on a handsome shawl, which an officer took possession of on the spot—an action which requires no comment.

The man behaved with great firmness. While the rope was being adjusted, a soldier struck him on the face; upon which he turned round with great fierceness, and said—"Had I had a sword in my hand, you dared not have struck that blow:" his last words before he was launched into eternity.

As Peel and I rode home to the camp, we agreed that it would have been much better to have conducted the execution with more decorum; and that such a display of jesting and greediness, and the careless off-hand way with which it was done, were more likely to make the natives hate and despise us, than to inspire them with a salutary dread of our justice.

It got dark before we arrived at the Naval Brigade camp, and that of the 53rd was at the other end of the plain. Of all the difficult things that I know, to find one's way about an encampment in the evening is the most so.

The rows of tents are all the one like the other, and few people know whose is the next encampment to his own, and hardly any one where an encampment at a distance off is, so that one can get no directions as to the way. Then in the evening, all the servants and camp-followers are cooking their suppers, and one's eyes are dazzled by the fires and blinded by their smoke, which, being that of green wood, makes them smart till they overflow with tears; then you stumble upon elephants picketed, who, as well as your horse, mutually hate and fear each other, and you can hardly get your horse to pass them; then camels, and bullocks, and bullock-hackeries innumerable; then interminable lines of cavalry and artillery horses, which you must go round—for if you went through them, you would probably be kicked to pieces—and in going round, you most likely lose your line of direction; and then the tent-ropes, occasionally extending beyond their proper distance, trip up your horse, and you find him on his knees, and yourself on your nose.

It took me two hours to go half a mile, and I only found my way at last by hitting off a road, and sticking to it, though the distance was three times as great as the direct road across the camp.

On another occasion I was more fortunate. I had been dining with the 9th Lancers, whose camp was on one side of Onoa, and that of the 53rd on the other. It being dark when I got to the part of the road whereabouts the camp was, I threw my reins on the horse's neck, and without the slightest hesitation he took me up to my tent-door! As Cowper says—

> Man, reasoning every step he treads,
> Often mistakes his way,
> While meaner things, by instinct led,
> Are rarely known to stray.

The following day we rode over to see Furrukabad and the Nawab's palace.

It is a very large and populous town, traversed by one main street, which occasionally widens into squares and open spaces. The distance between the two outer gates cannot be less than three miles, and it spreads on either side of the main street more than half a mile. The Nawab's palace is at the further end from Futtyghur, and is built upon a magnificent terrace, which formed part of a very large and strong native fort, though great part of the fortification is fallen into decay. He had set fire to it previously to decamping across the Ganges, and we found it a mass of burning ruins. The clothing department, which was in a part of the old fort, had fortunately escaped, and there were immense quantities of red cloth, &c. The authorities (I mean those during the mutiny) having got very hard up for money, and all the Bunneahs, or shopkeepers, having hid their stores of it, and all professing the most abject poverty, they (the Nawab and Co.) ordered a sale by auction of all this cloth, &c., and of course the tradespeople found plenty of money to bid for it.

They had to pay the money down as the lots were sold; and when it was all over the money was pocketed, and the cloth *returned into store*—pleasant sort of justice!

The terrace, which was very high, looked upon one of the most beautiful level views ever beheld. Immediately beneath it extensive gardens, fields, and woods, with mosques, tombs, and villas, peeping out from among the dark-green foliage; their elegant cupolas, and graceful minarets contrasting with the large heavy masses of the thick-leaved trees. These continued with undiminished luxuriance to the banks of the Ganges, whose smooth waters, reflecting the pure blue of the skies, glided in graceful sweeps through the whole length of the panorama. On the opposite side were wide sands of snowy whiteness, beyond which, far as the eye could reach, a sea of fields, groves, and villages, giving earnest, but for the desolation of war, of prosperity and abundant harvests.

The engineers had commenced mining the terrace and fortifications, which were soon afterwards blown up.

The townspeople were beginning to resume their usual occupations, and many of the shops were open; and in a short time the whole of the business of the town was going on as if it had not within a few months twice changed its masters. It is a great place for tent-making, and I purchased a very comfortable one, and turned my little dog-kennel over to Malakoff and his fellows.

A large force of engineers, and of working-people under them, were set to work to strengthen and repair the fort of Futtyghur, and to clear a space of eight hundred yards all round it, to prevent any foe approaching under the cover of the numerous houses and trees which were nearly up to the walls. On Thursday, 7th, the 82nd went out to recover some guns left on the banks of the Ramgunga, which were said to be the two which the Nawab had taken with him when he fled from the battle of the Kala Nuddee.

We met some peasants bringing them in; they were native-made, and very small.

Among the guns taken from the Nawab on that occasion were two 18-pounders, mounted on 24-pounder field-carriages.

It occurred to Peel that with a little alteration these carriages would do for his 8-inch guns, which he had brought up from the *Shannon* as far as Allahabad, and which he was very anxious to bring into the field; and, having got Sir Colin's permission, he set his artificers to work; very soon the 24-pounder carriage was converted into one for an 8-inch gun. He was much there while his people were at work; and, looking over the stores of wood already shaped out in the rough for gun-carriages, found a good deal which was sufficiently large and strong to make some more carriages for his 8-inch guns, and, with the assistance of Captain Legeyt Bruce, who was in charge of the gun-carriage department, before we left Futtyghur he had six nearly complete; and the same number of guns were telegraphed for, to Allahabad, to be sent to Cawnpore, to meet their carriages which we took down there on our way to Lucknow. Peel was particularly pleased at the prospect of getting his heavy guns, which he had brought up with so much trouble, into action, and of showing that they were just as capable of being worked in the field as the 24-pounders with which he had already astonished the army, and electrified and confounded the enemy.

We were for some time leading a quiet life at Futtyghur, very different from the excitement of continued marches and occasional skirmishes; and as the best weather for campaigning was rapidly passing by, we, and our betters still more so, were wishing for the immense convoy and siege-train from Agra to pass, and for the arrival of Colonel Seaton's column, which was also escorting an enormous convoy of provisions, and bringing some 4000 camels as baggage-animals for the army. Occasionally small expeditions were sent out to punish refractory nawabs or khans; but they usually managed to escape before we got up to their encampment.

Colonel Seaton's column was accompanied by a vast quantity of servants, a class of people till then very scarce, and difficult to get, for the immense number of new arrivals in India had absorbed all the spare ones down country, and the demand far exceeded the supply. Those who came down with Colonel Seaton were they who had belonged to the various officers, and others who had been dispersed by the mutiny.

I got a bheestie, one of the most useful, indeed absolutely necessary, servants in India; he was the ugliest little bandy-legged fellow I ever saw, but a tolerably hard-working little monster. When one's establishment has got two or three horses in it he has plenty to do, for he has to draw water not only for his master and the servants, and all the cooking, &c., but also for the horses, for they, or their syces, are much too fine to go to a tank to drink; but bheestie must bring it to them, and squirt it into a washing-basin or some such utensil, which the syce holds up to their

BHEESTIE PATCHOOLIE

London Saunders & Otley

mouths, and they suck in with the liveliest satisfaction.

On Tuesday, 12th, news having arrived that the enemy were in force at a village on the banks of the Ramgunga, and had broken the bridge, a brigade, under Colonel Walpole, with cavalry, artillery, and some of the guns of the Naval Brigade, were sent to oppose them, and to repair the bridge. On arriving there we found the bridge entirely destroyed, and that the enemy, whom we could see in considerable force about a mile from the opposite bank, had taken the greater part of the boats away, so that there were no means very handy of making another, though some eight or ten large country boats were shortly afterwards found two or three miles down the river; but as no serious attempt was ever made to bring them up, or to construct any kind of bridge, I suppose Sir Colin did not wish to have it done. We found one small boat near the pier of the old bridge hauled up in the mud, which Captain Peel launched, and sent a couple of ropes across to the other side, thus making a communication for the engineers when they should begin to make their bridge. In launching the boat we found a nest of snakes snugly coiled away under it; luckily they were all killed before they bit any one.

The two forces remained facing each other on the opposite sides of the river for nearly a month, occasionally exchanging a few shot, though with very little effect, for on our side the casualties only amounted to one Punjaubee cavalry man, and two bullocks! at least, I never heard of more. And I do not believe that the enemy suffered in a greater proportion, though we heard wonderful accounts of the numbers certain crack shots said they had hit.

Our doing nothing but observe them made the enemy very proud, and they said, that for a month they had stopped the whole force of the British army! Now that the plain is strewed with their corpses, and that our troops are in Bareilly, they have ascertained to their cost that they were not the insurmountable impediments to the British advance.

I used very often to ride out to that encampment to see what was going on, and occasionally took my bed, when Colonel Horsford, of the Rifles, an old friend of mine, and an excellent soldier, used to take me in and make me comfortable; it was a pleasant change from the dulness of the camp at Futteyghur, where there was nothing going on. There, at any rate, one might occasionally see the enemy, and hear the whiz of a shot, and so get up a little excitement.

Peel used often to ride over to see his detachment; and he set them to work to construct a raft of spars and empty barrels which would have transported fifty or sixty men, or even a field-piece, across, had it been required, and with the ropes which he had previously placed, would have made a very good flying-bridge.

However, it was never launched; therefore I conclude it was not then intended to cross the river.

On Monday, 25th, there were some garrison races at Futteyghur, and great fun they were.

Some ground was chosen near the camp, which was in good order and well-suited for the occasion. One course was level for the flat races, and another had several banks and ditches, with brushwood stuck on the top for the steeple-chases. There were several races and matches, and though neither the horses nor the riding were as good as on Epsom Downs, yet I daresay the spectators were just as much amused and excited, and plenty of money changed hands.

After the races were finished we got up a dog-hunt.

Some unfortunate cur is found, who is properly hallooed at, and who immediately cuts off as hard as he can put legs to the ground, and away we go after him, over banks and ditches, among groves and plantations, across the open and the fields, through villages; hallooing, shouting, laughing, tumbling down, scrambling up again, and all the varied incidents of the chase, till at last bow-wow is run into, gets one or two cracks with our hunting-whips, and is let go, and we draw the next village for another dog, and the same process is repeated until we or our horses have had enough of it.

On Tuesday night, while at mess, English told me that the 42nd were going a night expedition to catch some rebels who were encamped near a village called Mow, some eighteen miles north-west of Furrukabad; so I went to Colonel Cameron to ask his leave to accompany them. On returning I found the camp in the bustle of preparation, and to my joy heard that the dear old 53rd were going too.

The force, which was under Brigadier Adrian Hope, consisted of the 42nd, 53rd, a regiment of Punjaubees, Remyngton's and Blunt's troops of artillery, two squadrons of the 9th Lancers, and some of Hodson's

Horse. They mustered at the appointed parade-ground, and moved off at about eleven P.M., and marching to Furrukabad, defiled through its streets at midnight, and continued their march until about three, when they halted till daylight.

About six we resumed our march in a thick fog, which was very favourable to our purpose, as it entirely concealed our advance. At about eight we came to a large village, where we were informed that the enemy were encamped, to the number of 3000 infantry, and about 500 cavalry, with four guns, at a place called Shumshabad, which was three miles off. After giving the troops time to rest and to close up, we advanced, and soon came upon a large plain, and perceived their cavalry videttes and patrols to our front and on our right. Some of Hodson's Horse were pushed forward to reconnoitre, and word was soon sent back that the enemy was in force, and not far off; and on cresting a slight rise in the ground, we beheld their camp.

They had chosen a good natural position, and had strengthened it with trenches and batteries: it was on a gently rising ground, terminating abruptly in a cliff, some thirty or forty feet high, which looked upon a plain of great extent. On the left was a deep, though now dry, watercourse, which prevented the passage of cavalry or artillery, but over which, about a quarter of a mile in their front, was a stone bridge; their right had a slope down to the plain, which afforded them an easy escape. In the centre of their camp were some strong brick buildings, which were shot-proof—at least to field-guns—and a grove of fine large shady trees.

As soon as we came within reach of their fire, they opened upon us very sharply, and with very good aim. The artillery and cavalry were immediately ordered to the front, and away they went at a gallop —Hodson's Horse and part of the artillery crossing the bridge and taking up their position as in the plan, the Lancers and the rest of the artillery remaining on this side of the nullah—and soon the artillery opened a heavy cross-fire upon the camp with shot and shell, which it returned with considerable vigour.

Remyngton had taken up a position to the left and front of his guns, and I joined him, offering my services, if they could be of any use. After some time we observed the enemy's cavalry leaving the camp, and moving towards our left, under the cover of the

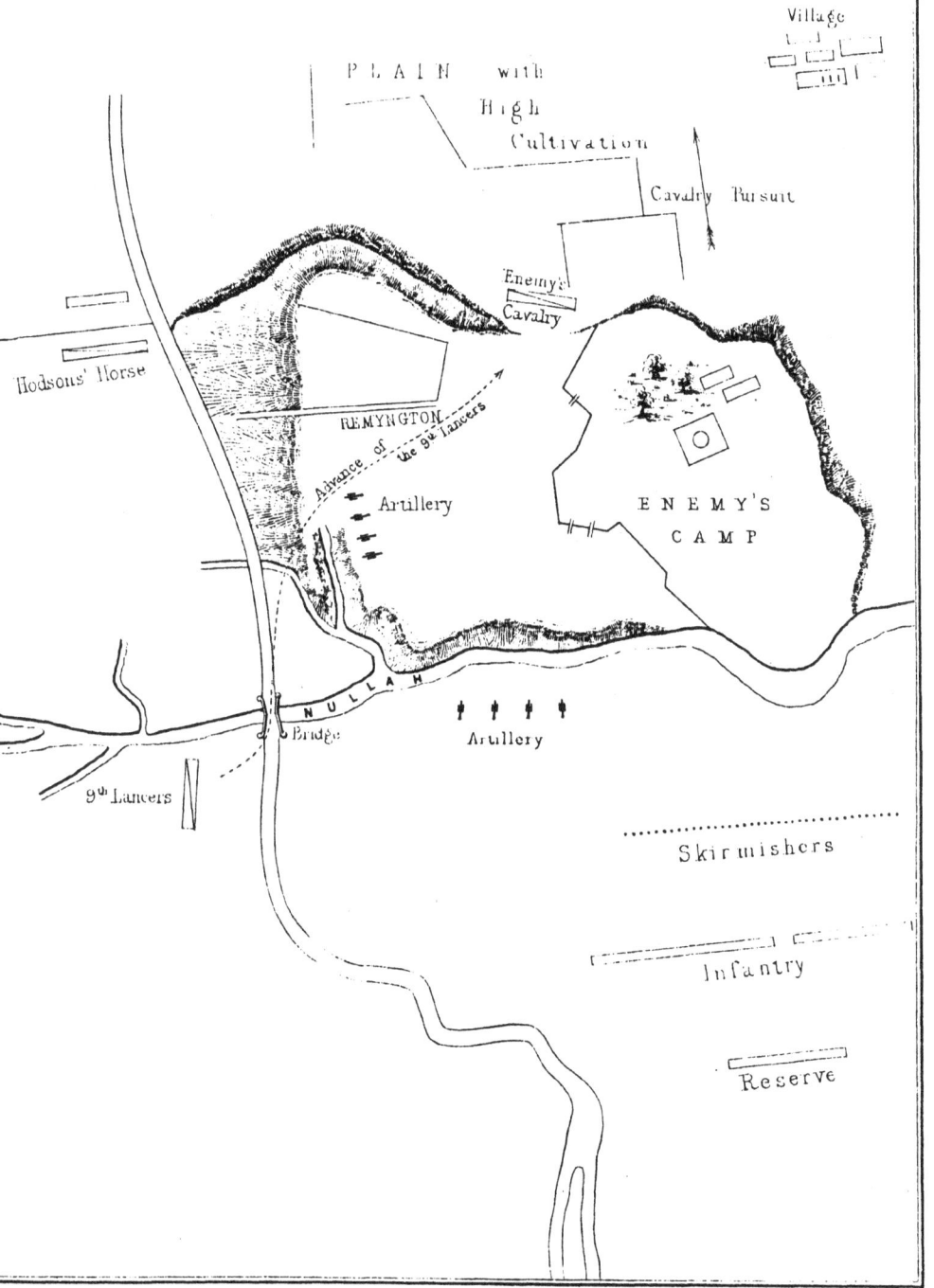

hill, and making towards Hodson, who, from the rise of the ground, could not see them. I galloped off to tell Hodson, and pointed out their heads, which we could occasionally see above the slope. He asked me, "Where are the Lancers?" who were on the other side of the bridge, and said, "Do go and get them." I galloped off, as fast as my little Arab could lay legs to the ground, to the Brigadier, who was bringing up the infantry, told him of Hodson's request, and he instantly sent his aide-de-camp to order them up, and away they went, and I with them.

Meanwhile Hodson had advanced under the hill, and had a skirmish with the cavalry, in which he was wounded in the hand. Some of his force behaved well, and seconded his efforts bravely, but a very large proportion held back till the Lancers came up to their support.

One squadron of the Lancers had to remain behind to protect the guns, but the other charged splendidly down the hill to the proper right of the camp, which was crowded with fugitives, and into the thick of the enemy, who did not stand the shock, but dispersed and fled in all directions; the rest of Hodson's Horse came up in the rear and joined the engagement.

As we came up with the enemy, I put my hand down to draw my sword, but to my surprise found the scabbard empty. In galloping it had jumped out—those abominable sling belts which look so pretty and graceful, are of no use in the field. As soon as one begins to gallop, the sword bangs about, sometimes turning right over, and falling out, as mine did. All the Irregular Cavalry men, who are allowed to choose their own appointments, have stiff leather belts without slings, keeping the sword firmly secured to the side.

It seemed fated that I should never take my sword into action; however, I had my pistols, and they did their share in the fight.

The cutting and hacking lasted some time, and some three hundred rebels strewed the plain, when the recall was sounded, and, looking back, we saw the hill and camp crested with the living wall of the infantry advancing with their skirmishers in front.

Brigadier Hope moved on rapidly about a mile, and then, as the enemy had vanished — Heaven knows where—halted his force.

While riding by him, his orderly came up with my sword in his hand, which he had found on the field, and, from the hilt being gilt, thought, no doubt, he had got a great prize, and brought it to his chief. I was delighted to regain it, for the blade was that of the sword which my father had used on the retreat upon Corunna, and I valued it much, and promised the man twenty rupees for finding it, which, when he was convinced that the hilt was not gold, and that it had not belonged to some swell khan or nawab, he was as glad to get as I was to regain my father's sword. He (my father) was so fortunate as to see a great deal of hard service early in his career, and was one of the youngest officers of every rank he held in the army; was Lieutenant-Colonel of the 18th Hussars at twenty-three, which regiment he commanded on the retreat upon Corunna, and which formed part of the rear-guard so constantly engaged with, and victorious over, the pursuing French, and he commanded the embarkation-guard when the army was embarked at Corunna, and was the very last man to leave the beach. He was a Major-General at thirty-five. Unfortunately for me, he died when I was not three years old, nor did he leave me any of his good fortune, for my career has been as slow as his was rapid.

A squadron of the 9th Lancers, and two guns, under Captain Johnstone, of the 9th Lancers, were now sent to pursue the fugitives to a ghaut on the Ganges, said to be eight miles off, but which we found much further; and Johnstone having orders to return before nightfall, reluctantly was obliged to retrace his steps without reaching it. We did not come upon any bodies of the enemy, though we could perceive them occasionally at a distance, skirting the plantations and cates of dholl, and endeavouring to show themselves as little as possible.

We got back to Shumshabad about six, and found the camp pitched on the rising ground in front of the enemy's old encampment, and as we had had nothing to eat since dinner the day before, were not sorry to see the mess dhoolie with a plentiful supply of prog and pale ale.

In this action there were several officers wounded, and a few men. Hodson in the sword arm and hand; MacDougall, his second in command, by a cannon-shot, which took off his leg—poor fellow! he died in the night; Captain Steele, of the 9th Lancers, was severely wounded in the hand and thigh, besides several slighter cuts, by a Sepoy, who first severed his bridle, and then, his horse being unmanageable, was able to cut his hand, and inflict other wounds; there was one of Hodson's Horse looking on, who did not offer any assistance, and who ought to have been hung could he have been identified. Captain Willis, of the Lancers, was also slightly wounded in the sword arm, and some others.

The natives are, many of them, excellent swordsmen; and when they turn at bay are most dangerous fellows, and generally leave their mark before they are killed. Almost all the crack cavalry officers, especially those of the Irregular Horse regiments, who are constantly having personal encounters, have some scars which tell of the desperation and skill of the rebels.

We captured the four guns which the mutineers had, and a considerable quantity of ammunition.

Unfortunately, we lost several men by explosions— one of a magazine in the encampment, and another by the blowing up of a captured tumbril which the 53rd were unlading. They had iron shot and powder all mixed together, and something struck a spark, which blew it up, killing and burning fourteen of the regiment. Almost all those who were badly burned died shortly afterwards. Captain Mowbray, who had his orders to go to England with invalids, could not resist the temptation of a last fight, when he heard his regiment was going on this expedition, and accompanied it, and very narrowly escaped losing his life by this explosion. He is a gallant soldier, and distinguished himself at Kudjrah, where Colonel Powel, of the 53rd, was killed, and where Captain Peel, succeeding to the command, gained a brilliant, though hardly won victory.

I was particularly pleased with my little brown Arab. It had carried me on its back from ten the evening before till six in the afternoon, twenty hours; had marched twenty-four or twenty-five miles to the field of battle; during the action no horse had more galloping about, and afterwards I rode it eight miles out and back with Johnstone's column of pursuit; and it was quite fresh at the end, and pitched into its gram with a gloriously good appetite.

After we had dined, we were glad enough to lay down to rest; and as we had brought no tents, Grant very kindly let us sleep in his dhoolies, and mighty comfortable things they are for a well and tired man; whether they would be as much so were one sick or wounded I cannot say.

CHAPTER VII.

RETURN TO HEAD-QUARTERS — ARRIVAL AT FURRIKABAD — AN INDIAN'S NOTION OF CHRISTIANITY—LIFE IN CAMP—MARCH TO CAWNPORE—A PIG HUNT—ARRIVAL AT CAWNPORE—MARCH TO LUCKNOW—ARRIVAL OF MR. RUSSELL—CAMP-FOLLOWERS—RACES.

NEXT morning, as it was ascertained that the enemy had all crossed the Ganges, and therefore our mission was attained, orders were given to return to head-quarters.

As a march at a foot's pace in the heat of the sun is not amusing, I determined to canter back by myself on a blood English-bred mare I had bought two or three days before, trusting to her speed if I should come across any stragglers of the enemy. On passing the spot where the enemy first opened upon us, there was a dead horse, now lying almost a skeleton, and near it some thousand vultures, far too gorged and lazy to do more than slowly and awkwardly hop out of my way as I rode through them. I reached head-quarters in two hours and a half without any adventure, but highly pleased with my purchase. When the country was open, and I could see around, I took it easy; but when the road passed through topes of trees, or any cover where a lurking foe might send, unseen, a bullet at one's head, I went by at a rattling canter.

I met Forster, one of the Chief's aides-de-camp, about half-way, going, with an escort of Irregular Horse, to get news of Adrian Hope's doings.

When I got to Furrukabad, where no doubt they had heard of the defeat and dispersion of the mutineers, every one was on their knees as I passed through the street; I never saw so much salaaming in my life. No doubt, had we been unsuccessful, they would all have spat in my face. I went to the Chief's tent, and told him what had occurred, and he was very glad at Adrian Hope's success.

The Chief's encampment was in a tope of trees, and a short way behind his tent was the most enormous bees'-nest I ever saw, hanging to a branch: it was a yard long, by about two feet wide, and the bees swarming upon and around it must have been numbered by tens of thousands.

About eight in the evening the force returned, having taken several hours to march the distance which my mare had brought me over in a comparatively short time.

The 53rd were mostly Catholics, I mean the men, and the church-parade for that persuasion was usually held in their camp. One Sunday, while that service was being performed, it so happened that I asked Malakoff what caste he was. He said, "I no caste, sar, I Christian."

"Oh, you're a Christian, are you? what sort of Christian?"

"I Catholic Christian, sar."

"Well, then, why don't you go to church? You see they are performing service now."

"Oh, sar, I no that Catholic; I no know that Christian. I eat meat, sar. I eat after master."

Which was the amount of his Christianity, and that of a good many others professing that faith.

One morning I found my establishment increased by an additional servant. I had been supplied with a bullock hackery and two bullocks; but when Colonel Seaton arrived with 4000 camels, they were taken away, and two camels supplied in their place. Next day I saw my friend the bullock-driver squatted in his accustomed place, and asked Malakoff what he was doing there.

"He leave bullock, he master's servant," was his reply. And he remained master's servant till master left India.

My days used to be spent at this time one very like the other. I used to get up about six, and saunter over to English's tent, and squat down on a box or chair, if there was one, and chat with him till it was warm enough (for the mornings in January and February are very cold) to have my musshack, and then perform my toilet.

A musshack is called so after the skin in which the bheestie carries the water. The operation is usually performed *al fresco* at one's tent door. Having reduced one's apparel to bathing costume, consisting of a very short pair of thick drawers, one squats down on a bit of board, and the bheestie proceeds to squirt the contents of his musshack or skin, which holds about two pailfuls of water, all over one; and a wonderful luxury and comfort it is, and marvellously refreshing. One's servants are all ready around to dry one and wash one's feet, &c. &c.

A MUSSHACH.

Soon after going to English's tent, he used to sing out for *chotter buckis* (which being interpreted, is little box, but which in reality was a corruption of his own of some uneuphonious name pertaining to his bheestie, which, doubtless, had a very different meaning).

On his appearance it was, "Chotter buckis, *gildie pellew* (make haste),will you, *dhood low* (bring milk) from the *buckrie* (the goat); and mind you *saff karew* (make clean) the mug well before you milk her;" which mixture, of what was intended for Hindostanee and English, was perfectly understood by the aforesaid bheestie, who soon reappeared with a mug foaming over with new milk from the goat, which, with the addition of the "*laaste* taste in life" of brandy or rum, made a good stomachic, and lasted very well until the mess-breakfast at nine or ten o'clock.

After breakfast, which was a substantial one, curries, stews, ragouts, cold meat, &c., being handsomely performed upon, I used to stroll over to the Naval Brigade camp and watch their parade, and the evolutions they went through; and it was astonishing to see how very well they performed, and with what steadiness they accomplished their marchings and counter-marchings, their forming squares, or advancing in line, the way they handled their arms, the regularity of their step, and their upright carriage. They looked more like a well-drilled corps than a body of Jacks, who, usually, cannot walk without rolling like a ship in the trough of the sea, nor stand without their legs apart at about the same angle as the shrouds of a seventy-four. It certainly reflected infinite credit upon Captain Peel and his officers, and upon the good-feeling of the men. The discipline was admirable; the men orderly, sober, clean, and respectful; and so great was the influence of Sir William Peel's high character and unflinching determination, that it was maintained with very little punishment.

When the parade was over, Peel and I and some of the officers usually rode to the fort to see the progress of the gun-carriages, or sometimes to Walpole's camp at the Ramgunga, then home to dinner, and about ten o'clock to bed, so that the time passed very pleasantly, especially that the weather was most charming; but we still wished and hoped for a move, for everybody felt that India was not to be reconquered by sitting still, and we knew that the temperate weather was soon to pass away.

At last, on Monday, the 1st of February, Colonel Seaton having arrived, and brought his immense convoy in safety, and Sir Colin having information of the siege equipage and convoy from Agra being well on their march to Cawnpore, the camp was broken up, and we commenced our retrograde march.

The Commander-in-Chief, with his staff, escorted by the 9th Lancers and some horse artillery, went by double marches, in three days, to Cawnpore. Our orders were to take seven days, and if we fell in with the Agra convoy, to halt a day, and allow it to get a march ahead of us.

Our column was under the command of General Grant, and the first day's march brought us within a mile of the Kala Nuddee. The skeletons and half-decayed bodies strewed by the roadside and over the plain showed where the fugitives had been cut up by the cavalry. I felt much interested in going to the different points where we were on the day of the battle. The bridge had been properly repaired while we were at Futtyghur, and was as good and as strong as it had been before it had been burnt.

On Wednesday we halted about eleven o'clock at Jehallalabad, near Kanooge, and a pig-hunt was got up by General Grant and his staff, and they asked me to accompany them. About twenty elephants were sent out an hour before we started to get to the ground in time. Our way lay through Kanooge. As we rode along, the General pointed out to me the scene of his fight there, and of the pursuit of the discomfited rebels. We crossed the Kala Nuddee to get to the ground, which was on a tongue of land between it and the Ganges—the confluence of the rivers being about four miles lower down.

The ground was much more favourable to pigs than to pig-*stickers*, for it was covered with very high grass —sometimes over the horses' heads—and very few open spaces.

The elephants were marshalled in line about twenty feet apart, and we rode on some forty or fifty feet in front of them. Very soon there was a cry of "Soo-ur, soo-ur-burra soo-ur" (pig, pig, big pig), and away we went at a gallop, forcing our way through the long grass, our horses clearing the higher tufts with immense bounds; luckily, the ground was tolerably soft and even, so that we had not many falls; for it was perfectly blind riding, one could not see the ground a yard before one.

A PIG HUNT

London, Saunders & Odey

In our gallop we came upon a litter of pigs. I heard a tremendous rush, and my mare gave a jump as if she would have flown over the moon, and I saw one of the pigs disappearing under her stomach into the long grass. We seldom kept a pig in sight more than two or three minutes. The only one killed was a squeaker, which, in its youthful inexperience, took to the open, and was hotly pursued by those who saw it break, General Grant leading; and we had a splendid burst for ten minutes, when, just as piggy had reached the friendly covert, and in another moment would have been lost to our anxious gaze, a great black greyhound, which was one of two dogs which accompanied us, caught it by the hind leg, and instantly a spear was in its side, and poor piggy's blood bedewed the plain.

On our way back we turned up a fox, and had a twenty minutes' course after him across the open, at the rate of forty miles an hour; however, he got away from us, and piggy was our only trophy.

I particularly admired General Grant's riding; he went as fast as a three-year-old, and he and his horse seemed to be almost parts of the same being, so firmly and gracefully did he sit it.

We arrived at Cawnpore on the 7th (Sunday). I rode on before the column, and beat up my friend Cannon, who was Brigade-Major there, for a breakfast.

The bridges over the Ganges were covered with artillery, and ammunition, and stores of all kinds, which formed long lines far as the eye could reach, slowly wending their way towards the city of Lucknow.

Sir Colin, we heard, had gone to Allahabad to consult with the Governor-General, who had made that place his head-quarters, so as to be in nearer communication with the army.

About noon our column had all arrived, and the camp was pitched. When I got to the 53rd, I found to my great joy that my kind friend English had got his Lieutenant-Colonelcy, and that Gore, Dalzell, and Prince had each got a step in the regiment. Maybe we did not have a big drink that night! I believe every man in the 53rd was delighted at the winner of Chuttra, where the 53rd gained such laurels, getting confirmed in the command of the regiment.

Our encampment was near that where Sir Hugh Wheeler made so gallant a stand against many thousands of the mutineers.

It is perfectly marvellous how they could have held

out so long: there was not a square yard on the whole of the buildings which did not show the mark of a ball; and the entrenchments which surrounded it were so slight—mere scratches in the earth—that a man could have leaped over them with ease. No doubt the rains had washed them partly away, still they never could have been but of the very slightest description.

One day news came in that the 88th had had a successful engagement with the Calpee rebels, in which Thompson, one of the four survivors of the Cawnpore massacres, had been wounded.

On Thursday, 12th, we got our orders to march towards Lucknow, and early on Friday morning the regiment was in motion, and moved off across the bridge of boats, and marched to Onoa, the scene of two of Havelock's victories.

Orders reached us to halt here instead of proceeding at once towards Lucknow, and we encamped about two miles beyond Onoa, on a large level plain.

We heard that the Chief had received some intelligence which caused him to delay for a few days the advance upon Lucknow. News also came of the arrival in the Chief's camp of the talented representative of the *fourth estate* of the realm, Mr. Russell, the

Times' correspondent, and that he had been graciously received at head-quarters.

It had been doubted by many whether the Chief would have liked to have had a reporter always at his elbow; but there is no man to whom such a person could be less inconvenient than to Sir Colin, for he always kept his own counsel, and there was no place where so little was known of the future movements of the army as in the head-quarter camp, so that it was impossible for any one to give any information which might do harm if it got into the enemy's hands; and every one who knows Sir Colin must be aware that the more the things that he has done are correctly reported, the more will they conduce to his credit and redound to his fame. Mr. Russell being with the army is a great boon to the good people at home, as they get from mail to mail a very interesting and correct history of the events of the war as they occur, and also of the feelings and thoughts of many of the people engaged out there, and many stirring incidents are recorded which, but for his graphic pen, would never have been known beyond where they took place.

The encampment around Onoa was a very large one,

as the immense parks of artillery and ordnance stores for the reduction of Lucknow had been massed here, and the enormous quantity of ground covered by the army and its belongings is incredible, and would not be believed out of India.

A division of the army, and that not a very large one, moved from one side to the other of Onoa, a distance of two miles, and it took eight hours from the time the advanced guard left the old ground till the rear-guard arrived at the new encampment; true, they were escorting a large part of the siege train, which, besides the guns and mortars, had carts upon carts of ammunition, each drawn by five bullocks, which again required carts upon carts more, also drawn by five bullocks each, to carry food and fodder for these numberless bullocks. The Naval Brigade, for instance, which had only sixteen guns—but they are monsters—and ten rocket tubes, had no less than 800 bullocks attached to the guns and their belongings.

Besides bullocks, there are elephants, camels, horses, ponies, "tats" (a miserable kind of pony), goats, fowls, geese, &c., and camp-followers innumerable, and yet not a quarter of what there used to be before Sir Charles Napier commenced his reforms of the establishments which formerly accompanied a force of the Indian army in the field.

Even now every officer has from four to twelve servants, and the men also have several attached to each company, for a private in India cannot draw his own water, nor cook his own victuals, nor could he, till lately, clean his own boots, nor shave his own chin, but shoe-cleaners and barbers were attached to each regiment.

There is a bazaar also which follows every corps, and which is under the control of the commanding officer. It supplies all the things which are required by soldiers on a campaign, such as soap, tobacco, &c.; also gram for the horses, a kind of vetch, which is their principal food, and which they much prefer to oats; and many other things which it would be very inconvenient to carry about with one.

Officers, even the Commander-in-Chief, who in this, as in everything else, sets a good example to his army, now live in what is called a staff-sergeant's tent, which is not more than 12 feet square, and these, in the junior ranks, are tenanted by two, and sometimes three officers. They can be carried by one large, or two small camels, whereas formerly every officer

MY ESTABLISHMENT.

London Saunders & Otley

had a large tent, which required four or five camels to carry it, and those of the field-officers were almost as large and luxurious as a good house, and of course required a proportionate number of elephants or camels, and their attendants.

The number of servants every officer is obliged to keep in India is a great addition to the impediments of an army, especially where food has to be carried, as was the case in Oude. No one tried to do with fewer than I did, but I had got up to nine, and had I remained in India much longer, I should have been obliged to have two or three more.

True that five of them belonged to my horses, for usually every horse has its groom and grass-cutter; I made two syces do for three horses; but for myself, I had Mr. Malakoff, who was as good as two or three, for he was cook, butler, valet, and first-lieutenant; a coolie, a bheestie, or water-carrier, and a dhobie, or washerman, and a camel-driver, who had two camels in charge. The grass-cutter sallies out at early daylight, provided with an instrument not unlike a bricklayer's trowel in shape, though one edge is very sharp, with which he scrapes up the grass close to the earth; and it is marvellous what a quantity he will collect from ground as brown and burnt-up, and apparently as innocent of any herbage as the bare palm of one's hand.

The grass which the horses prefer, and, indeed, which is best for keeping them in condition, is very dry, short, and crispy, almost resembling moss, which he shaves off the ground, roots and all. Should the grass-cutter bring any of a coarser or longer description, or any with the slightest appearance of greenness, the syces — who would not himself cut a blade of grass for your horse were it starving—would most certainly reject it, and send the grass-cutter for more, and very likely give him a good licking into the bargain.

There certainly is a good deal of club-law among the natives; and every one of them thinks he has a right to *wop* any other who is the least beneath him in caste, situation, or service; but I can truly say that I saw very little, if any of that kind of thing from officers to their servants; indeed, I do not think I ever saw an officer strike his servant; and though, no doubt, the cases my good friend Mr. Russell mentions are strictly true, yet that kind of performances are the exception, and by no means the rule.

All these servants are not so serious an expense as it might be thought, for their wages vary from twelve to four rupees a month, for which they have to feed and clothe themselves. I found that my nine servants and three horses did not cost me more than one fine young gentleman, who did me the honour to call himself my groom and valet, and one horse did in England.

Besides my horses and camels, I had a goat and half a dozen fowls, which gave me a plentiful supply of milk and eggs; it was a curious fact, that these beasts and birds always knew their own tents and belongings, and never strayed to any one else's domains, nor did other people's, and some had pigeons besides the fowls and goats; but they always kept to their own master's tent. The hens were very particular when and where they chose to lay their eggs. Sir William Peel had one which selected a corner of his tent, behind a particular portmanteau, and used to produce its daily *ovation* soon after the march was over and the tent pitched, but never would do so until the portmanteau was placed in the proper corner.

My first question every morning to Malakoff usually was about the eggs, and he used to tell me, " hen give one egg,—give two egg," as the case might be. The cock who was lord and master of my six fowls was an early riser, and every morning before daybreak, when one was having one's most delicious sleep, made a point of coming to my tent, just by the head of my bed—canvas walls do not keep out much noise—and setting up the most uproarious cock-a-doodle-dooing that ever was heard. I used to wake up in a rage, and roar out, "Malakoff, there's that cock again; take it away and strangle it." Presently a rushing would be heard of Malakoff chevying the cock, and loud flutterings and suppressed crowings.

By-and-bye, when Malakoff appeared in his capacity of valet, I used to say, "Well, have you killed the cock?" "No, saa; suppose killum cock, hen no give egg;" and so he was daily condemned and daily reprieved, till I left him a living and crowing cock when I took my departure from the camp.

The servants are generally of different castes, and will neither cook nor eat together; nor indeed will they let one another, still less their masters, approach their cooking-places. One day, while my syce was cooking his dinner, one of the officers took a bit of burning wood from the fire to light his cigar; of course the dinner was defiled, much to the grief of the syce, and to the benefit of the Matey, who, being the lowest of the low, eats after anybody, and, I believe, after everything, and who was soon demolishing the savoury currie which the indignant syce turned over to him.

Their kitchen and *batterie de cuisine* are very simple; they scoop out a hole in the ground, about eighteen inches long by twelve broad, three sides of which they surround with a little mud wall about six inches high, in this they make a little fire with a few chips and two or three bits of dried cow-dung, which is much used for fuel in India; around this fireplace they sweep a space of about five feet across, which they keep clear, and which forms a sanctuary which no one not of their own caste can pass without defiling the victuals; two or three lotahs, or metal pots, are their cooking utensils, and with these small means it is astonishing what good things they will produce.

In addition to the servants, &c., belonging to the officers and regiments, there are ten dhoolies attached to each hundred men; each dhoolie having five (four and a spare one) bearers, so that a regiment has from four to five hundred of these people with it. Also, the field-hospital of the force has a small army of dhoolies and dhoolie-bearers. And moreover, and above all these, there is the commissariat, who have to carry provisions and necessaries innumerable for the forces, and whose beasts, servants, &c. &c., nearly double the "impedimenta" of the army; yet it must be said of it that it is the most wonderfully organized department; and it had only to appear in Orders that such a division was to march to-morrow at daylight with a month's (or whatever time might be stated) provisions, and by the time denoted every camel, elephant, or bullock-wagon would be in its place ready for the march—a state of perfection seldom attained by the commissariat of any country.

It can be easily conceived what difficulties these armies of camp-followers, and servants, and multitudes of animals add to those of the movements of troops, and how much they increase the cares of the Commander-in-Chief, and hinder his movements and operations. Indeed, it may be truly said, in the language of the Emerald Isle, that "the army is the *laaste* part of itself."

While at the encampment near Onoa, the Naval Brigade got up some races, which were great fun.

There was every description of race—horse races,

NAVAL BRIGADE RACES

London, Saunders & Otley

pony races, flat races, hurdle races—foot races, flat and hurdle—leaping in sacks, and, to wind-up, there was a buffalo race, with two Jacks on each, and a half-dozen other Jacks pushing, and shoving, and pulling at the buffaloes' tails to make them go, and go the right way.

As may be supposed, there were plenty of falls and tumbles, from the captain downwards; but, as no one was hurt, it all passed off well, and was capital fun.

After the races were over, which was not till past sunset, I cantered over to the 53rd's new camp, which was at Gopie Gunge, about five miles nearer Lucknow, where they had marched that day; and after an hour's hunt in the dark found my tent. Troops had arrived there from different directions, and a force of about three thousand were assembled under General Grant, and were to march the next morning on a "dowr" to clear the country north of the Cawnpore and Lucknow road of insurgents and followers of the Nana, who was said to be in some stronghold about twenty miles off.

Before dawn the next morning (Tuesday, 16th February) the camp was in motion, and soon the force was formed upon the road, and after retrograding a couple of miles, turned off to the northward,

K

and followed a country road over an extensive plain. There were various reports of the enemy being seen, and one officer, whose eyes were better than mine, pointed them out to me by thousands, though I confess that I could not see one.

After marching about three hours, a staff-officer came galloping from the front, and reported that a swell had been seen on an elephant, escorted by many Sowars, making off across the country.

Some troops of cavalry were immediately ordered in pursuit, each troop taking rather a different line of country. I went with one of the 7th Hussars, under Captain Slade; and away we went at a gallop for about five miles, though without seeing either elephant or Sowar; at last the men and horses having had galloping enough, were halted, and, after resting a short time, we quietly retraced our steps to the main body of the force. One of the corporals of the 7th had a pet monkey, who sat on his shoulder the whole gallop, and seemed to enjoy and relish the fun very much.

On regaining the column we continued our march without interruption to a large village called Jamatnugger, beautifully situated upon the banks of a rippling stream, where we encamped for the night. Soon the camp was hushed in sleep, for our march had been very fatiguing the last few miles, having been across country, without any road, which made the advance very slow and tedious.

CHAPTER VIII.

SKIRMISHING AT FUTTYPORE — JAGGERMOW — BANGHURMOW — NEAR OF THE NANA — TAKING A "SHORT CUT" — STORMING OF MEANGUNGE — CAPTAIN STEWART — SCENES AFTER AN ENGAGEMENT.

EARLY next morning we were on the move, and marched to Futtypore, passing through Safferpore, a large town, which was nearly deserted, and where the cavalry had a chase after some Sowars. At Futtypore, which was a strong fort belonging to an ally of the Nana, but which we found deserted, the 9th Lancers cut up about twenty fellows, who were escaping, and took their chief, who was an agent of the Nana, and had letters from him upon his person, ordering him to evacuate the fort, and to take with him some guns, which, however, he had not had time to do, and which we found there. In riding round the town after the cavalry, I saw Anson dig a fellow out of the high dholl, with his arms, and take him prisoner; soon afterwards, seeing a *donkey* in the dholl, I thought that there was something else, and on cantering up, sure enough there was an old scamp and his family. I made him give up his arms by the cogent persuasion of a revolver at his head, and come along with me; as he tried to bolt, and gave me a chevy, doubling like a hare, when I caught him again I took him in tow by the hair of his head, and made him walk by my side; however, I thought it would do no great good taking the old fellow up to camp, where he would probably have been hung, having been captured with arms in his hand, so giving him a good kick in the seat of honour, I told him to *jow*, and he was off and out of sight in some thick plantation in the twinkling of an eye.

I gave his sword to one of the troopers of the 9th, who seemed glad to get it; it was silver-mounted, and I dare say a good one.

When we got back to the camp, General Grant hailed me to join them at breakfast, which was spread out most invitingly under a large shady tree, and most kindly wished me to join his staff-mess, which, as I was already in that of the 53rd, I declined; still on this dowr he or some one of his staff constantly asked me to dinner and breakfast, and I experienced from them all the greatest kindness. The breakfasts were particularly welcome; they had a capital mule, who carried it, and who was always up with the advanced guard, so that directly we halted a shady spot was chosen, and in five minutes an excellent repast was spread out, whereas the regimental meal was often not ready for an hour after our arrival. General Grant was always glad to have me riding with him or his staff, which was a great pleasure and advantage to me; indeed, there is no one in the army in India to whom I am more indebted for friendship and consideration than I am to him.

On Thursday the force halted, but a detachment was sent to Jaggermow—a strong fort six miles off. We found it deserted, fortunately for us; for it was large, with thick mud walls, which would have stood the battering of our field-pieces for ever. The fort was burned and blown up, so that when the rebels returned to it—which no doubt they did as soon as we had left the coast well clear—they could have found nothing but smouldering ruins and shattered walls. I rode back by myself, and found that the fort and town of Futtypore were in flames, the first of which blew up with a grand explosion soon after I reached the camp.

On Friday, the 19th, we marched to Banghurmow, and on approaching it were met by a deputation begging for mercy to their town, which, as it had been friendly to us, was spared, and orders were given to prevent its being plundered, or the inhabitants being molested; notwithstanding which, in a few hours there was a good deal of looting going on, which, when reported to the General, a little of the provost-marshal's cat to the soldiers, and plenty of *bamboo back-sheesh* to the camp-followers, soon put a stop to it, and this salutary punishment prevented any more plundering during that dowr.

The march of the next day was the limit of our path northwards, and we crossed the dry canal, which had been cut some centuries ago to connect the Ganges and the Goomtie at Lucknow, but which was never finished, as it was found that the difference of level would cause too great a stream; and in those days locks were not understood in India. We encamped beyond it, and here we got news that the Nana, with the Nawab of Cawnpore, and three other chief rebels, was at a fort ten or twelve miles off, with some 6000 men, and that he intended making a stand. As it was being talked over, some one of the staff said, "What a glorious bag they would make;" General Grant said, "Yes; but we must obey orders;" and no doubt his instructions from Sir Colin were so precise and particular as to prevent his going any further, even with such a prize in view. No man in India would have been more likely to succeed than he, for to carefulness and circumspection he adds in a remarkable degree that promptness and dash which seize the right moment for an attack on the enemy.

The next morning, Sunday, the 21st, we commenced our march to rejoin the Chief's camp.

While loading one of my camels, the other bolted off, and it was an hour before he was caught, so that the force was some little distance on its march before I got away, and had nearly crossed the canal. I thought to take a short cut, instead of going round by the road, and came to a path down to the canal, bad enough, but got down safely; on the opposite side it was perpendicular, so I rode along for half a mile till a path, up which some goats were straggling, appeared, and up which I tried to ride my mare; but when she was about six feet up, she lost her footing, and fell over the little cliff, down on the whole length of her back, and it was fortunate that she made such a complete somersault, or she probably would have broken her neck or legs, had she fallen on them. I found myself —I knew not how—on my feet, quite clear of her, and what was most strange was, that neither she nor I was the least hurt; the only thing which came to grief was a bottle of sherry which I had in one of my holster-pipes. A little way further on I found another path, not much better, which I rode her up, notwithstanding my syce's remonstrances, and which she scrambled up with the activity of a cat.

On the 23rd there was a rumour in the camp that the enemy was in force at the fortified town of Meangunge, and, on joining the General on the march, he confirmed it. Intelligence had been received that they were there to the number of 2000, besides some cavalry, and that they meant to make a stand.

When we arrived near it—a strong guard being left with the baggage—the General took the force away to our left, so as not to approach the town too near until he had reconnoitred it, and determined where to make the attack. Meangunge is a long oblong, with the old Cawnpore and Lucknow road running through its length, and surrounded with a high loop-holed brick-wall, with circular bastions at the angles, and at convenient distances along the sides.

The gates were strongly fortified, with bank, ditch, and palisade in front of them.

We could see a great many people, armed, on the walls and bastions.

General Grant, with his staff, rode forward to reconnoitre, and we soon saw a considerable body of the enemy's cavalry, but they retired as we advanced, and when they saw what a considerable force we had, scuttled off, and were no more seen.

As soon as the General had settled where to breach the walls, the heavy artillery, consisting of a long 18-pounder and an 8-inch howitzer, were ordered up; they had elephants harnessed to them, and though brought up as much out of fire as possible, yet I saw the General casting wistful glances at them as they advanced, for had a stray bullet hit one of the elephants, he would probably have bolted off with the gun, and we should not have seen it again for some time. Fortunately, they came up without accident, and glad we were to see the huge beasts unharnessed, and marched off to the rear. The cavalry were sent round to intercept any fugitives; the infantry drawn up where they were, at hand, but under cover from the fire of the fort; the light company of the 53rd, under Captain Hopkins, thrown forward in a plantation which approached the walls near enough to check the musketry fire from the fort; and some Punjaubees to the right of the guns in another plantation.

About a couple of hours' pounding brought down a piece of the wall large enough to let four men abreast enter, when the 53rd were ordered up to be ready to assault, and the General spoke a few encouraging words to them.

As they marched by, Payn sung out to me, in his cheery voice, "Are you coming in with the 53rd, old boy?"

They marched to the plantation, where their light company was, ready to give the assault; meanwhile Turnour's troop of artillery came up in the most splendid style, and opened a heavy fire all along the face of the wall, to clear it of the enemy. Soon Anson was sent to order the 53rd to the assault; the cannonade ceased, and they immediately debouched from the plantation, headed by their gallant colonel, and marched as steadily as if on parade towards the breach.

When I saw them about half-way, I put spurs to my horse, and cantered up to them just as they came to a large sheet of water in front of the walls, and joined Anson, who, with his love of fighting, had gone on with the 53rd to the assault, and we, dashing through the water side by side, were in a minute through the breach, he beating me by a neck. Luckily the niggers did not wait there for us, but fled; in a second the leading files of the 53rd were up, Hopkins getting first to the breach, and turning to our left down a street, we were directly among the enemy, chopping and sticking as hard as we could. In the skirmish I got a sabre-cut on my right hand from a Sepoy whose thick skull I had just laid open, but who cutting nearly at the same moment, caught my hand before I could recover myself. An officer shot him with his revolver, and he and half-a-dozen others, who were in a little enclosure about fourteen feet square, were soon lying transfixed with the bayonets of the 53rd. Hungerford, one of the assistant-surgeons of the 53rd, bound up my hand, which soon became stiff and nearly useless. About this time poor Brockhurst, of the 53rd, was shot through the body; he lingered two months, and when I left Lucknow there was every hope of his

IN THE SKIRMISH I GOT A SABRE CUT ON MY RIGHT HAND FROM A SEPOY WHOSE THICK SKULL I HAD JUST LAID OPEN

recovery, but I have heard since that he died, much regretted by his noble corps and all that knew him.

We now advanced, headed by English, rapidly through the streets (Payn had meanwhile taken the left wing through the fort to the right of the breach), the enemy flying before us, but occasionally making a stand for a moment, and firing from some place of concealment, and we soon came to the Lucknow Gate, through which they were rapidly escaping. A great many also bolted into a large serai or khan, which, to their misfortune, they found to be a *cul de sac*, and where they were all killed to a man.

As the enemy were all bolting, and we were afraid that those outside might not observe them, and my disabled hand preventing me from being any more use inside, I offered to go to the General and tell him what was done; and retracing my steps through the town and breach galloped off to find him; but as he had moved on, I informed Colonel Hazard, commanding the cavalry, and he, soon seeing a cloud of the fugitives escaping, let loose his fellows at them, and a great many were killed. In every direction, for the General had closed every exit from the fort, the enemy were met, and routed with great slaughter, of whom I bagged two with my revolver with my left hand. Some of them made a desperate resistance; a little knot of them got round a tree, with their backs to it, and defended themselves long, until they were all slain. One brave fellow, seeing the Lancers after him, faced round with his sword and shield. Captain Coles, of the 9th Lancers, rode at him, and sent his lance through shield, body, and all; but the fellow in falling made a swinging cut, and ham-strung Coles' horse, which was obliged to be shot. Cornet John Evans, of the 9th Lancers, killed no less than eleven men with his own hand. I saw one of these footmen standing at bay, surrounded by six or seven irregular cavalry, who were all, evidently, afraid of him, and in the twinkling of an eye he rushed at one of them, cut him off his horse, and then slashed him as he lay on the ground, so that he lost both hands; but while thus employed, another rode at him with a lance, and ran him through.

About two the action was over, and the pursuers recalled. General Grant and his staff, among whom I figured that day, as he kindly put me down as his extra aide-de-camp in the return of wounded, assembled under a spreading mango-tree to refresh the inner man with our breakfast, but which we had a narrow escape of being done out of, for the cloud of fugitives came by the place where the mule and servants were, and they, consomers, kitmutghurs, bearers, &c. &c., all bolted, and left the old mule by himself. Fortunately the fugitives were in too great a hurry, and had too much to do to look after themselves, so the old mule was left alone, and presently, after they had passed, the servants came back as bold as brass, and we got our breakfast as comfortably as if it had not been surrounded and in peril of capture by the enemy.

Next day we remained encamped at Meangunge while the town was being destroyed and the gateways were being blown-up by the engineers. I rode into it with Captain Stewart, of the 35th; he was with the General, but was appointed to General Lugard's staff, and had joined this dowr pending the arrival of his chief. He was an old friend of mine, and we were very glad to meet again, especially during such interesting times.

Of the many talented men I have met in the army, I have not come across any man more so than Captain Robert C. Stewart (now, I am happy to say, brevet-major) of her Majesty's 35th. He knows English (I hope), French, Italian, Hindoostanee, Persian, Birmese, and I don't know what more in languages; plays well on the cornet, draws well, understands photography, is a good mathematician, a good surveyor and observer; and when, on his passage home the captain and mate could not manage their lunars, he put them to rights in quick time, and worked them out for them correctly. It is not every soldier who can show an old sea-salt the way on his own element!

The sight in the town was not a very pleasant one; corpses strewed about in all directions, some of which had been burned, and were peculiarly horrid-looking. I saw only one woman's body, and that was of an old lady of eighty or ninety, who was lying dead by the mouth of a well, but who, I suppose, died of fright, for there was no wound nor mark of violence upon her. It must be said that, very much to the credit of our soldiers, they never hurt the women nor the small children, though of course, occasionally they got killed, for bullets and shells will hit them as well as men, if they get in the way.

Though there is nothing so exciting in the world perhaps as the shock of battle, nor is there a greater pleasure than to see your enemy go down—especially by your own hand—yet it must be confessed that the scenes which present themselves the next day give one very different feelings, and sometimes individual cases of distress are most heart-breaking. One of great sadness may be here adduced: Roberts, the Assistant Quartermaster-General, was giving directions about burning a part of the town, when an old, infirm man, who was sitting at the door of a house, entreated him to spare it, saying "that yesterday morning he was the happy father of five sons; three of them lie there, pointing to three corpses; where the other two are God only knows; that he was old, and a cripple, and that if his house was burned he would have nothing left but to lie down and die." Roberts, who is as good as he is brave, gave directions for sparing the old man's house; and I hope that the two missing sons have escaped, and have returned to comfort his few remaining days.

CHAPTER IX.

MONOA—A BRAHMIN BULL—MARCH TO LUCKNOW—SIR COLIN CAMPBELL—AN IRISH DISCOVERY—THE CUSHLA MAKREE OF THE KING OF OUDE—REACH LUCKNOW.

NEXT morning we broke up the camp early, and marched to a place called Monoa, about twelve miles off, and where there was an old stone bridge which crosses the same stream which is spanned by the Bunnie-bridge some way further down. Some opposition was expected there, as it was a place which a few determined people might have defended for a long time against a very superior force, but the licking they had got two days before at Meangunge was quite a sickener for them, and there was not a musket fired at us.

The following morning we crossed the bridge, and encamped on the extensive plain which stretches from there to Lucknow, with scarcely a rise or fall in the ground of twenty feet. The camp was pitched about two miles beyond Monoa, and strong pickets were thrown well out, as it was quite possible for the people in command at Lucknow to detach a large force to attack us.

Captain Evans, who accompanied our force, and who had been Assistant-Commissioner of this district, went to examine the house of the great man of Monoa, who had taken an active part against us in the insurrection. He found in it not only the cutchery tent and floor-cloth pertaining to his magisterial office, but some of his own chairs, tables, and furniture.

In a shed, tied up, we came across a little Brahmin bull, which, as soon as he saw us—not being accustomed, I presume, to European faces—became perfectly mad, and made the most violent attempts to get itself free, in which it had just succeeded, when I gave it a barrel of my pocket-revolver—without which I never moved—which brought it to a stand-still, and presently it expired, to the great horror, no doubt, of the bystanding Hindoos, who certainly looked aghast; but I could not afford to be knocked over and gored to please them or their prejudices.

We remained encamped here two or three days, awaiting orders from the Chief.

My hand was beginning to get a little easier. For the first three or four days it swelled up as big as a child's head, and was very painful; but constantly keeping the bandages wet made it much easier. When I was riding, I made my syce, at every well we came to, draw a lotah full of water and pour it over the hand. At first I slung it in a black silk handkerchief, but I soon found that the sun striking upon it made the pain intolerable, so I substituted a white one, which afforded instant and great relief.

At last, on the 1st of March, the order came to join the Commander-in-Chief's camp, which was at a place about eleven miles from the Alumbagh, and we started about one P.M. Our march was much delayed by a small but deep stream, which was very difficult for the artillery and ammunition to cross, the bottom being muddy and uneven. General Grant, as was his habit when any difficulty occurred, remained to direct and accelerate the passage, yet it was night before it was entirely accomplished.

In the morning, long before daybreak, the camp was in motion and the army filing along the road to Lucknow, and covering several miles of it. The baggage was not allowed to advance until a great portion of the army was on its line of march, and it looked like a great sea of men and beasts on either side of the road.

On the march I again met Captain Peel and his Naval Brigade: he was delighted to see me, and congratulated me upon getting off so easily as I had, with only a clip on the hand; he seemed to think that it was a very lucky thing to get wounded, and I rather agree with him that an honourable scar is worth having. He was in great spirits at the thoughts of soon having his monster guns in full play at the devoted city of Lucknow. About noon we came to the encampment near the Alumbagh, where Outram had so long repelled the attacks of his countless foes with the small army of heroes under his command, and there I first saw him. He was talking to, and taking leave of Sir Colin.

Sir Colin received me very kindly, though he good-naturedly shook his fist at me, and said—

"You got that poking your head where you had no business," pointing to my hand in a sling.

I dare say he was alluding to an order of his, which

I knew nothing about, disapproving of staff officers and aides-de-camp putting themselves at the head of regiments when there was anything daring to do. I had no idea of doing anything of the sort, but merely cantered past as the 53rd was advancing, and what a man on horseback can always do, got quicker to the breach than they could. My only feeling was pretty much what Sir Charles Napier said a soldier ought to have, a wish to stick my sword up to the hilt in the first Sepoy I met, and, thank goodness! I did run one fellow through before I was disabled.

Some time afterwards, when Sir H. Havelock's despatch recommending his son for the Victoria Cross was much canvassed, I asked English if he had felt annoyed at me, or thought me in any way presuming in what I had done? "No, my dear Jones," was the noble-hearted fellow's answer, "that never entered my head; the only thing I felt was fear lest you should be killed." And I am sure, from the many kind things said to me on the subject both by the officers and men also of the glorious 53rd, that there was not one who blamed me the least for what I had done.

Sir Colin is certainly a marvellously strong and enduring man; no amount of work and fatigue seems to have any effect upon him. A couple of days before he had ridden from Lucknow to the Alumbagh, and back to the camp near the Bunnie Bridge, a distance of between fifty or sixty miles; and that in an Indian sun, is what few men could go through without great exhaustion and fatigue. I am told his staff had quite enough of it, and that he was quite fresh. There are few qualities in a General of more importance than being able to go through a great amount of exertion without knocking up, and that Sir Colin possesses, among many other great qualities, in a remarkable degree.

Our line of march now diverged to the right, and leaving the Alumbagh on our left, we took the road to Jellalabad—a strong post held by our pickets. Here the Engineers had been very busy preparing fascines and gabions for the siege, also bridges made of spars and empty casks, which were intended for the army to cross the Goomtie by. After leaving Jellalabad the way was by a baddish road, with high dholl fields on either side, and when the head of the advanced guard debouched from it into the open plain, some distance to our left of the Mahomet Bagh, they saw the enemy in position, before a tope of trees, who immediately opened fire upon them from some guns.

The artillery belonging to the advance guard came up at a gallop, and forming up in splendid style, unlimbered, and returned their fire with interest. Part of the cavalry also went off to their left to take them in flank.

Soon the head of a regiment of infantry was seen issuing from the narrow road at a quick pace, and forming up as it got on the plain, upon sight of which the enemy decamped, leaving their guns behind them.

Soon after they had retired, a regiment of native cavalry was seen coming from the place where they had been, and, for a moment, was thought to belong to the enemy, and the guns were turned upon them, when Sir Colin, whose eye is not easily deceived, after gazing at them a few seconds, said—" All right; they are our own people!" thus preventing what might have been a sad mistake.

This little skirmish, which lasted about an hour, cost a few casualties, but not many, as the enemy did not await our closing with them.

Afterwards, when a considerable part of the force was brought up, we turned to the right, and took the direction of the Dilkooshah, which we found unoccupied, and took possession of.

It is curious what queer discoveries are sometimes made by our brethren of the Emerald Isle. An Irish major being told that the meaning of Dilkooshah was heart's delight, exclaimed—" Oh, then, sure there must be the same derivation for the Hindoostanee and the Irish; they have Dilkooshah, which means heart's delight, and have not we our Cushla Makree!"

The Martiniere also was unoccupied, but when the enemy found we did not take possession of it, they reoccupied it, and established a battery at its eastern corner, which we could not effectually silence until the Martiniere was assaulted.

Brigadier Little, of the 9th Lancers, was wounded by a Sepoy who had concealed himself in the Mahomet Bagh, who fired at him and hit him in the arm, near the elbow, which deprived the cavalry of his very valuable services.

The Dilkooshah Park, which, when Sir Colin relieved Lucknow, had been covered with fine trees and luxuriant grass, affording cover for numerous deer and other game, was now quite bare and parched up, and the greater part of the trees had been cut down.

The palace, in which a strong picket was immediately placed, was as a house in good preservation, but all its furniture had been removed, and there was nothing but tarnished gilding and frames of immense pier-glasses, the fragments of which were lying about, showing that it had once been the "heart's delight"— the "Cushla Makree" of my Irish friend—of the King of Oude.

Meanwhile the army was gradually coming up, and the Quartermaster-General's department were marking out the camp, which was placed in rear of the wall of the Dilkooshah Park, with its right resting nearly on the Goomtie, and its left extending some two miles, and facing the Mahomet Bagh and the parks and gardens to the south of Lucknow. Sir Colin, having made all necessary arrangements, had his breakfast spread out under the wall of the park, and he sent an aide-de-camp to ask me to join him, which I did with great pleasure; a good breakfast in those circumstances being a thing not easily got, and by no means to be despised.

In the afternoon some of the Naval Brigade guns and some of the heavy siege guns belonging to the Artillery were got into position on the brow of a hill

SIR Wᴹ PEEL BRINGING HIS GUNS UP IN FRONT OF THE DILKOOSHAH.

to the right front of the Dilkooshah. Peel, as was his custom, leading his guns, and perfectly indifferent to the balls which occasionally struck the ground within a short distance of his feet. A couple of Peel's guns were posted near the corner of the wall of the Mahomet Bagh.

The enemy fired occasionally, and an unlucky shot mortally wounded two of the Naval Brigade, one of whom, Terry, by name, had been an old shipmate of mine in the *Hannibal*, in the Black Sea. His thigh was shot off, and he died in the night; but the other man, whose skull was smashed, and a piece of which, as large as half-a-crown, was sticking in his brain, did not die till three days afterwards.

At length we were in front of Lucknow, with every prospect of our hopes for months past being realized.

There we saw, gilded by the rays of the setting sun, her golden domes, her slender minarets, her squares, her palaces, her earthen ramparts, raised by immense labour within the last three months, pierced by thousands of loopholes, bristling with many guns; and within the protecting circle of which were, we knew, from fifty to one hundred thousand of those wretches who for months had vainly endeavoured to conquer the unconquered garrison of the Residency, which had been snatched from their grasp by the genius of Colin Campbell, and who soon were to be driven headlong from their stronghold with slaughter and ignominy by that same commanding spirit, and by the daring and valour of the soldiers and sailors he led on to victory.

CHAPTER X.

PREPARATIONS FOR THE SIEGE—THE DILKOOSHAH—MR. RUSSELL—PASSAGE OF THE GOOMTIE — THE BOMBARDMENT — SIR W. PEEL WOUNDED—THE ASSAULT OF LUCKNOW—SORTIE BY THE BESIEGED.

THE following morning we heard of the near approach of Frank's column, who had accomplished a victorious march from Benares to Lucknow, during which he had beaten the enemy in several engagements, capturing the greater part of their guns and killing and wounding a great number of them. He had been deficient in cavalry, and had mounted some few cf his regiment (the 10th), who made excellent light cavalry men.

We also gained intelligence of the advance of Jung Bahadour with his Gourkas, and that they would arrive in five or six days, and we earnestly wished for their appearance, as we knew that the principal operations would not be carried out without them, from reasons of policy rather than from any want of their assistance.

Meanwhile the Engineers were busily preparing two bridges to throw across the Goomtie; and immense numbers of gabions and fascines were got ready to form the batteries which were soon to open upon the devoted city.

For the first two or three days there were several marksmen placed upon the roof of the Dilkooshah to keep down the fire from the Martiniere, but it was found to be of little use, and that it drew a fire constantly upon it, which, as it was an excellent station for observing the enemy, was obviously inconvenient; therefore orders were given that no one but those on duty should be allowed to go up there, for it had become a rendezvous for the idlers of the camp.

I found one morning a sentry on the stairs, who told me his orders were not to allow any one to go up who was not on duty, and as I could not make out the slightest case, I was obliged to go back.

However, I did not relish being done out of my look-out place, so I went off to General Mansfield, and begged him to give me an order to go up there. At first he demurred, saying that it was no use giving an order to break it immediately, and if he gave it to me, he would have to give it to others; but I pleaded that post-captains in the navy were not so plentiful in the camp that they might be picked like blackberries off every bush, and I got my order. Just as it was given to me in came Mr. Kavanagh, of Lucknow celebrity, who had come to join the army as a volunteer, to see the capture, as he had been through the siege, and who was seeking the same indulgence as I had got, and which he also obtained, though not without a slight growl. We returned together to the Dilkooshah, and, presenting our orders, were permitted to ascend; and certainly it was much pleasanter for the indulged, for there was room to move about and to see well, which there had not been before.

I was very glad to meet there my friend, Colonel Harness, who had been recalled from Calcutta, where, much to his grief and vexation, he had been sent after the battle of Cawnpore, to organize and send up efficiently the men of his corps who should arrive in the country, for he was more anxious than most men to signalize himself in the field, which he did in the operations in advancing from Bank's bungalow to the Begum's palace, from the Begum's palace to the Imam Barah and Kaiserbagh. No man nor officer was more constantly to the front, nor was any one more assiduous and constant by night and by day in directing the sapping and mining operations, by means of which those strongholds fell into our hands.

On the top of the Dilkooshah I also first saw and had the honour to make acquaintance with Sir Archdale Wilson, the conqueror of Delhi, and I found that it was his elder brother, Captain George Knyvet Wilson, who had been an old captain of mine for several years, one whom I much looked up to, and for whom I have always felt a sincere friendship.

Among others whom I met up there and chatted with for several days before I knew who was my acquaintance, was a very agreeable, intelligent, good-natured, stout, middle-aged gentleman, dressed in the carky colour worn by half the army, and who I concluded to be an engineer officer stationed there to observe the movements, &c., of the enemy.

It was not till I had got quite intimate with him and looked out regularly to have a yarn with him for some days, that one of my friends said to me, "Do you know who that is you have just been talking to?" "Not the least idea," says I. "Dear me! why, that is Mr. Russell of the *Times*."

One evening, as Mr. Russell and I were riding

home from the Dilkooshah, a shot from the Martiniere battery very nearly put an end to the delightful letters from "Our Special," and these ill-digested, ungrammatical, and rather nautical recollections of mine. We saw the flash, and presently heard the whiz, which increased most unpleasantly in intensity, till plop went the ball close beyond us; it could not have passed two feet from our heads, and had our horses made one step less, it would have knocked them off. A little experience tells one exactly the direction a shot is taking; directly the report is heard, the whizzing follows it. If the whizzing does not increase very rapidly, you may be sure that it wont come near or trouble you; but when you hear it like running up the chromatic scale with the greatest crescendo fortissime, till it attains almost a screech, then look out for your eyes and limbs.

En passant, I may observe that I do not believe in the wind of a shot doing the least harm—that and several others have passed pretty near my head, and more than one has covered me with dust, and I never felt the slightest breath fan my cheek. Unless it grazes, however slightly, it has no effect whatever.

Captain Peel also often spent an hour on the top of the Dilkooshah. News had just arrived of his being made Aide-de-camp to the Queen, and also K.C.B., and every one was delighted at his unusual merit and gallantry being rewarded.

Alas! for how short a time was he to enjoy his well-earned honours.

There was not much doing for four or five days. The Chief's camp had to be moved back a quarter of a mile, as the shots from the enemy occasionally plumped into it. One passed through Sir David Baird's tent just after he had left the spot; and another whizzed among three officers of the 42nd, one of whom was the chaplain, though without touching them.

On the 4th and 5th the engineers were employed throwing the bridge over the Goomtie, and on the afternoon of the 5th I walked down with Sir William Peel to see how they were getting on. Major Nicholson, the most hardworking man in the world, was there, placing them; and as he had only native sappers with him, he had to do great part of the work himself. Peel offered him the services of some sailors, which he was glad to get, to attend the ropes, &c., as they could understand what he wanted, whereas all his orders had to be translated to the natives, a proceeding which neither accelerated nor facilitated the operation. However, he worked hard, and had his bridges ready by the time they were wanted.

The next morning, the 6th, Sir James Outram, with a large force, of all arms, at 4 o'clock commenced the passage of the Goomtie. Sir J. Hope Grant was with him in command of the cavalry, and I was soon in his wake.

The force took a long circuit, partly to be out of the reach of the guns of the Martiniere, and partly to escape the observation of the enemy.

When we had proceeded some miles, and had brought the town to bear in the direction that Sir J. Outram required, our right shoulders were brought up, and we advanced in line, at least the cavalry did. Before we had proceeded far, the advanced guard sent word to say that the enemy were in front, horse, foot, and artillery, and we soon saw them like a great white cloud dotted with red, nor did they appear to me to be in any regular formation. We now advanced rapidly, but when within about a thousand yards of them they broke and fled, and away went our cavalry after them at a gallop, the artillery following as fast as they could. The broken nature of the ground, as we advanced, it being seamed with nullahs, soon disturbed the regular formation of the troops; and the Bays, anxious to signalize themselves in their first action, galloped down the road which ran through the plain, and part of them, led by Major Percy Smith and Captain Seymour, pursued the fugitives right up to the walls of the inclosure in which they had taken refuge. Here Major Smith was shot dead, and our foremost horsemen were obliged to retire. Captain Seymour, and some troopers of the Bays, endeavoured to bring off his body, but they were attacked by so many of the enemy that they were obliged to abandon it, Captain Seymour carrying off his helmet, sword, and medals, and being the last man to leave the spot, except an unfortunate corporal of the Bays, whose horse would not allow him to mount, and who was literally cut to pieces. A corporal of the 9th Lancers also endeavoured, ineffectually, to recover the body of Major Smith. I heard him relating to General Grant what had occurred, and one of his aides-de-camp, poor young Havelock, who since has been killed, offered to try and fetch it in, and went off with a dozen troopers, but soon returned, saying that it was impossible, as it was surrounded by so many of the enemy. In the advance I saw my friend Captain Anson attack and kill a Sowar; how many more he polished off I don't know, but he clearly has a peculiar vocation for splitting niggers' skulls.

The cavalry was now recalled, and the artillery kept blazing away for some time. At last, Sir J. Outram having decided where to encamp, which he did on the Fyzabar road, about three miles from Lucknow, the troops were marched back to their ground, pickets thrown out, and the work for the day was over.

A troop of Lancers and two guns went back as a convoy to Brigadier Napier and other officers, and with an account of the day's work to Sir Colin, and I took advantage of it to retrace my steps. We took a different route from that by which we had come; indeed, nearly a straight line, and passed through some awkward enclosures and sand-hills, which were very difficult to get the guns over, leaving a village on our right, which had been that morning full of the enemy, but which was now untenanted by any one but a few old women and cripples.

As soon as we passed this difficult ground, and had

reached the open, Mr. Kavanagh and I cantered on, and soon reached the head-quarter camp.

After I had had some refreshment, and that most luxurious of Indian luxuries, a musshack, I repaired to the Dilkooshah, and met there Mr. Russell, who had been watching the movements of the force all day, and he pointed out where the Bays had reached. They and all of us in the skirmish had thought that they had charged up to the very walls of Lucknow, but it appeared that they never were within a mile and a half of it, and that the enclosures where they stopped were near Chinhunt.

The next two days there was not much done on our side, except a constant interchange of shots between the town batteries and ours, without any great result on either side; but Outram made considerable advances, and on the third day had got his batteries into position, so that he could shell the Kaiserbagh and other palaces, and also could fire behind the line of defences which the enemy had thrown up along the bank of the canal from Banks's house to the Goomtie. Their ideas of fortification are very primitive, for all their defences were made as if they could be attacked from one point only, and they had made no provision for resisting any attempt to force them from any other direction.

On the morning of the 8th, hearing that Sir Colin was going over to Outram's camp with an escort, I thought to take advantage of it, and do the same; and some time after the troop of the 7th Hussars who were to accompany him had marched to headquarters, I got on my mare, and rode down to the bridge over the Goomtie, but seeing no escort, trotted quietly on. After going on about a mile, and still seeing no one coming, I concluded that they were either gone on, or that there was some delay, and that they were not coming, and as my mare was a fast one, and I knew that—barring accidents—very few Sowars could catch her, I went on alone, and took a straight line across country. On rising a slight eminence, I saw a long string of people, with their bullock-carts and so forth, moving along from Lucknow, and out of sight of both camps. After looking at them a moment, I saw an officer among them in an European costume, and concluding they were some people, camp-followers, &c., belonging to Outram's force, cantered on; but when I got within a couple of hundred yards, I saw that the officer was a Sepoy, and was at once aware that they were on the wrong side. However, not liking to go back, I determined to chance it, and putting spurs to my horse, I went through them as hard as I could gallop, and to my surprise and pleasure also, was not fired at, nor indeed any way molested. I suppose they were people escaping from Lucknow, and their object was to do so as quickly and quietly as possible; if they had begun firing they might have had some of our cavalry upon them, which would not have suited their book at all. Soon afterwards, passing a village and some unpleasant enclosures, I came upon the plain on their further side, and the first person I met was Sir Hope Grant, who was reconnoitring a way to get the heavy guns up into position to enfilade the canal defences, without their being exposed to the enemy's fire in their advance. When he had completed his survey, we returned to his camp, and there met Sir Colin, and while he and the Generals went forward to reconnoitre again, I went with General Grant's staff to a capital breakfast; they might have stuck up over their tent, "Good entertainment for man and horse," for one never went near them without oneself and one's beast being well taken care of.

On the 9th, Franks being up, Jung Bahadour near, and Outram having gained a position so as quite to enfilade the defences, Sir Colin began the capture of Lucknow in earnest, and orders were given that the Martiniere was to be taken that day. Soon after daybreak several powerful batteries of artillery, which had been placed in the night, opened upon it in every direction.

Sir William Peel had several of his guns in position, and they soon commenced a rapid and destructive fire. I offered him my services during the siege as aide-de-camp, and he gladly accepted them.

The Naval Brigade had some eight or ten rocket-tubes, 24 and 12-pounders, and some were on the right of our battery. In the relief of Lucknow, Sir William Peel told me, out of 140 rockets (I think is the number), only one did not go truly to its destination. On this occasion they did not behave so well. The sticks had got too dry, and caught fire, and away went the rocket anywhere but where it was wanted; and the composition had also got too dry, and burnt so quickly, as, in many cases, to fall or explode far short of their proper range. Whether it was an older batch of rockets, or whether their having been exposed to the sun for some months was the cause of their misdoings, I do not know, but they were a great failure; and Sir William Peel was as much surprised as annoyed at their uncommonly bad behaviour.

While the guns were upon hard ground—which it was in the Dilkooshah Park—they were worked with great ease; but afterwards, when we had possession of Banks' House and the first line of defence in Lucknow, the soil of the batteries was so soft and sandy, that it took immense labour to run up and work the guns. All manner of expedients had to be adopted— sandbags placed under the wheels; planks, doors, shutters under the trails; and as these had to be renewed or altered each round, considerable time was wasted; and from the wheels often not being quite level, the balls did not go as truly as they ought.

We had a good deal of trouble, also, with some of the shells; especially those supplied for our 8-inch howitzers; they were joined to the wooden disk, which prevents their turning in ramming home, by a tin cylinder, which embraced the disk and half the shell. A great many got loose, and turning in ramming home, the fusee got inwards, and gave us great trouble in getting them out and ramming home

WINTER CAMPAIGN IN INDIA. 171

again; in some cases it was impossible, and they had to be fired as they were, and burst in or close to the muzzle of the gun. (I may as well inform my readers who are not initiated into the mysteries of gunnery, that we always keep the fusee of the shell outwards, in which case, when fired, it lights, but is not otherwise disturbed, and burns steadily to its destination; whereas, should it be inwards, and against the powder, the explosion blows the composition right through the fusee, and bursts the shell at once, to the great danger and peril of those around, and the waste of ammunition and labour.)

Another thing which caused considerable loss of time, labour, and ammunition, was, that many of the fusees—especially the wooden ones, which had probably been a long time in store—burnt too quickly and irregularly, and many of the shells burst long before they had reached their intended destination.

We also saw very many of the shells which were thrown from Outram's batteries bursting in the air far from the Kaiserbagh and other buildings which they were directed at, evidently from the same cause.

It would be a wise precaution if all fusees made beyond a certain date were burnt, and none issued which had been long enough in store to be deteriorated. The wooden fusee is not an expensive article, and the metal ones could be refilled; and though a certain expense would be incurred, yet, as a pounds, shillings, and pence question, it is only sacrificing a penny to save a pound; for every faulty fusee used causes a shell to be thrown away. The waste of ammunition in the field, where it often cannot be replaced, the confidence the comparative harmlessness of the fire gives the enemy, and the tendency the want of success in firing has to render the artilleryman unsteady and careless in laying and aiming his gun, are serious evils.

Notwithstanding these *contretemps*, the work went on well and merrily in the batteries; and any deficiencies in material were fully made up for and compensated by the zeal, intelligence, and exertions of the officers and men.

Soon after the cannonading began, Colonel Napier pointed out a wall that he wished breached, and Sir William Peel ordered up two more of his guns, and selected an excellent position to place them in, some way to the left and front of the other battery; and when they were in position, and had opened fire, he went to a place about fifty yards more to the left, to watch the practice made by his guns.

The wall of the Martiniere Park was some two hundred yards nearer than the wall we were breaching, which was part of the enclosure of the palace itself, and in front of the park walls were several rifle-pits. Peel, with his usual indifference to danger, thinking only of the effects of his shot against the breach he was making, and taking no notice of the bullets which were buzzing about our ears, was standing upon a little knoll, a fair target to the marksmen. One could see the fellows lay their muskets along the top of the rifle-pit, then puff, a little white smoke; then bang, and whew-ew-iz, then sput against some stone as the bullet fell flattened close to our feet. At last one bullet, more true than the others, struck him, and he fell, saying, "Oh, they've hit me!"

I saw that he was hit in the thigh, and was stooping down to bind it up, but he said, "Go and get some help;" and seeing that there was no flow of blood from it, I ran to the battery, and told Lieutenant Young of it, asking him to take some men to carry him off, and then ran to the Dilkooshah to get a surgeon, who immediately came with me, and we met

Peel being brought up. On examination it was found that the bullet had not touched the bone, or any vital part; and after it was extracted, the surgeon said it was not a dangerous wound, and that in about six weeks he would be able to move about. Alas! in little more than that time he fell a victim to a dreadful disease. Far better for him would it have been to have expired with the sound of his cannon ringing in his ears. There is no death so glorious, so much to be desired, as on the battle-field.

That evening he was taken to his tent, where I went to see him after the day's work was over, and I found him cheerful and doing well.

About two, the cannons having well done their part, the assault took place, and the niggers not liking the look of the Highlanders, 53rd, and Sikhs, as well as some Horse Artillery, after a very feeble defence, took to their heels, and retired behind the ramparts on the canal, whence they opened a heavy musketry fire from their thousands of loopholes. In front of this canal my friend Captain Robert Stewart was wounded in the foot. General Lugard expressed a wish to know whether the canal was dry or not, and without further order or hint, Stewart gallantly dashed out to the brink of the canal, and ascertained what his General required, under a tremendous fire, and while doing so was struck on the foot, but galloped back and made his report.

Soon after, the enemy finding that they were enfiladed by Outram's guns, left their defences on the banks of the canal, which were immediately taken possession of by the Highlanders and Sikhs. During the night there was an attempt made by the Sepoys to regain some of the ground they had lost, but a withering volley thrown into them at half-range altered their plans effectually, and sent them howling to the right about.

In the morning there was a battery of the Naval Brigade guns placed at the corner of the Martiniere Park, to breach the wall of the compound of Banks's bungalow, and some mortars, served by the artillery, were constantly throwing their shells in the same direction.

Presently we saw the plumes of the Scotch bonnets waving along the ramparts, as they advanced carefully in skirmishing order towards Banks's house, and soon afterwards seeing them close up to it, the firing ceased, the breach having been made, and they rushed in and took possession of it with very little opposition.

So far the carriages made by Sir W. Peel for his 8-inch guns answered admirably, but they were some of them beginning to show signs of weakness in the trunnion-boxes; the other heavy field artillery had iron plates on the top of the brackets of the carriage, which descended into the trunnion-boxes, so that the trunnions worked upon iron, but at Futtyghur, Sir William, being pressed for time, and also there being some difficulty in forging such heavy ironwork, did without the plates, thinking that as there are no plates on our ship's carriages they would do as well without them on shore as on board ship, and I thought the same. However, he found in practice that the constant firing shook the hind part of the trunnion-box so much that they had to make iron plates to insert between the trunnions and the worn-out part of the trunnion-box, which answered pretty well as a temporary expedient.

CHAPTER XI.

ATTACK ON THE BEGUM'S PALACE—A SAD ACCIDENT—GALLANT CONDUCT OF A HIGHLAND PIPER—CAPTAIN MACBEAN—JUNG BAHADOUR VISITS SIR COLIN—ASSAULT THE IMAUM BARAH AND KAISERBAGH—ESCAPE OF THE MOULVIE.

SIR WILLIAM PEEL had now given up the command of the Naval Brigade to his first lieutenant, James Vaughan, and I begged him to make me useful to him in any way he chose.

Soon after possession was obtained of Banks's house the naval guns were brought forward, and part of them placed in battery to the right of it, in rear of an embankment, which only required some embrasures being cut to make a capital parapet; and two others, under Lieutenant Salmon, were got into a garden on the right of the road, which led up to the Begum's palace, which was the next place to be taken.

Lieutenant Young commanded the battery near Banks's house, and a better officer never existed; the heavier the fire he was under, the cooler and steadier did he become, setting a good example to his men; indeed all the officers of the *Shannon* were men of the first stamp, and Sir William Peel often told me that though he had had nothing to do with choosing any of them except his first lieutenant, that if he were offered the pick of the whole navy, there was not one there he would change for any one of his officers.

As soon as the guns were got into position, a heavy fire was opened upon the Begum's palace and the defences in front of it; the enemy's fire of cannon was soon nearly silenced, and they retired behind their second line of defence, which was in front of the Begum's palace, and of a serai on the opposite side of the road, and then turning backwards, joined the next line, which was in front of the Kaiserbagh; they kept up, however, a smart fire of musketry from the hundreds of loopholes with which it was pierced in every direction, and occasionally sent a shower of grape down the street.

As I was carrying a message from Young's battery to the other, my horse was struck in the chest by a bullet, but which must have previously hit something else, the ground or a wall, for it only cut the skin and raised a big lump; however, it made her jump like a two-year-old.

I met Sir Colin and his staff in the evening as they were returning to camp, and he kindly said to me—"You have done good service to-day!" and on more than one occasion afterwards he spoke to me in the most flattering manner. I need hardly say that his good opinion and praise are invaluable, and most gratifying.

The next morning the Secunderabagh fell into our hands. Intelligence was brought to General Lugard, commanding in the town, that it was unoccupied by the enemy, and he instantly set off with some troops, and took possession of it. He had hardly done so when a heavy column of the enemy was seen approaching it; but when they saw the red-coats inside, and got a few admonishing shots, they turned tail and retraced their steps.

General Lugard had taken up his quarters in Banks's house, and thither Sir Colin and his staff went. While they were standing in the verandah a shot struck Fred Flood of the 53rd in the leg; he was acting aide-de-camp to General Mansfield at the time.

After that some sandbags were put up, which at

any rate made one's legs safe, if it did not one's shoulders and head.

Meanwhile the fire from the batteries upon the Begum's palace was kept up unceasingly. There was a tree in front of one of the naval guns in the right battery which was very much in the way. Vaughan, with one of the carpenters, went out and hewed it down, and fortunately they escaped unhurt, though there was a sharp fire from the enemy's loopholes upon them. It was a very daring act.

There were four bungalows, called the D bungalows, from being so marked in the plan. By degrees the enemy's sharpshooters had been driven out of them, and we held the two nearest to our battery, the two others were neutral ground; but from the loopholes of the serai opposite a sharp fire was kept up on them, as it overlooked them, and any people who showed themselves had a very fair chance of being hit. A Sikh— and I must say they were always among the foremost wherever danger was—was mortally wounded by my side, and there were several other casualties.

Brigadier Napier, seeing that the breaches in the Begum's palace were nearly practicable, determined that it was necessary to breach the serai also, so as to storm it at the same time, and told Vaughan to get two guns into the compound of the most advanced D bungalow that we held, and make a breach through the two walls of the other compounds, and then through the wall of the serai, which was accordingly done. A battery of small mortars was also placed to the left of our guns, which poured their shells rapidly into the Begum's palace and the serai.

Here we had a sad accident. A fine young fellow, called Garvy, a mate of the *Shannon*, came down with some message to Vaughan on horseback, and, as he turned to go away, rode in front of the mortar battery, which was on the road of the compound leading to the gate. Just before he passed, the quick match with which they are fired had been lit; the officer in charge of the battery called to him, but too late—the mortar went off just as he passed, and knocked his head clean off. He was a most amiable, fine young man, and his unfortunate death was much deplored by all his messmates and friends.

Soon after we had got our guns ready, Adrian Hope, whose brigade was to storm the Begum's palace, came to see how we were getting on, and as we had two walls to clear away before we could breach the serai, it was feared that it would take some time, but one or two shots soon showed that 8-inch balls at 100 yards would go through all three, and we had the satisfaction of seeing a way beginning right through them all. Vaughan gave me one of the guns, but unfortunately, after a few shots, the trunnion-box being worn, the gun jumped out of it, and slipped down to the ground.

Another gun was wanted from the park, and the triangle to mount the fallen one, and more ammunition; and as there seemed a probability of the assault not taking place for some little time, and my horse was handy, I offered to take the orders up to camp.

I always brought my horse down as near the batteries as I could, and looked out for some safe corner to put him in; and as there was nothing to loot, and besides bullets were flying about, I knew my syce was not likely to budge from his cover, and I was sure to find the beast when I wanted it.

My little Arab seemed quite to understand that I was in a hurry, and never went quicker in its life, and in a very short time I had been to the camp, and was back again; but I found that Vaughan had made such good use of his remaining gun, that a large breach was opened through the serai, and that the assault was just given, and the Highlanders were swarming into the Begum's palace.

Vaughan with a dozen of his best shots had advanced opposite the breach he had made, and was keeping it clear, and keeping down the fire from the loopholes in the serai.

At this moment Colonel Longden, of the 10th, but attached to Franks' Goorkahs, came forward with some of his men, so I thought I might as well go also, and cut across the road, down the ditch, and up the other side (how I managed I can't tell, for I had only one available hand), and with the others rushed through the breach. The enemy did not wait for us, but bolted. Soon part of a regiment marched in through the gate, and afterwards a regiment of Goorkahs. The fighting was still going on fiercely in the Begum's palace, and the Sepoys were bolting in all directions, and our fellows after them.

In the gate of the serai I saw the body of one of the officers of the Highlanders lying on a charpoi, and several others of the soldiers.

Several Sepoys rushed out in the street, but they

were instantly cut or shot down; some got into small places opposite, and as we crossed over after them the enemy opened from the batteries in front of the Kaiserbagh a precious peppering of grape, canister, and round-shot down the street. At our end of the street, between the Begum's palace and the serai, was a battery, which of course was deserted by the enemy. It occurred to me that if we could get some guns up on the road, on the other side of it, they might silence these gentlemen whose fire was sweeping the street. So I went back to propose it to Vaughan, but found that he had anticipated me; he was bringing up one of his guns, Young was bringing up another, and they soon opened a fire in return upon the Kaiserbagh batteries. As they had to fire over the rampart, they could not see their object, and had to point their guns partly by guess, so I took my station on the parapet, and directed them, telling them how their shot went. Young came up, too, but Vaughan called him down, as "he was wanted in the Naval Brigade, and it was no use getting knocked on the head that way;" the shot, round and grape, were certainly coming pretty thickly around us. After about half an hour's firing—all our shots plumping into their battery—they were silenced, and we ceased firing; and when I came down I received congratulations from all hands at having my head on my shoulders.

When the Highlanders advanced to storm the Begum's palace, they found a deep ditch in front of it, which they had great difficulty in getting over, and lost a good many men in effecting it. A piper, who was among the first to get across, as soon as he was landed on the narrow footing between the ditch and the wall, under a tremendous fire, struck up a national pibroch, strutting up and down as only a Highland piper can strut, and much encouraged his fellow-soldiers to exertion and daring by his soul-exciting strains.

One of the officers, Captain MacBean, of the 93rd, killed no less than eleven men with his own hand. I heard Adrian Hope telling the tale—MacBean, after recounting the deed, added, "I never struck a man in anger in my life before." He struck sharp and well when he did strike.

There was a very considerable slaughter of the Sepoys—some 700 were buried next day—many of them fought with desperation, but they could not withstand the bayonet thrust by the strong arms of the Highlanders.

That day Jung Bahadour had arrived, and paid a visit of ceremony to Sir Colin, which prevented him being on the spot to see the capture of the Begum's palace. His troops were soon brought into play, and began working their way into the city of Lucknow, to the westward of the line of palaces.

This day, also, Outram made a considerable advance, seizing the approaches to the iron bridge, and establishing himself all the way from the Badshah Bagh to the river.

In fact, this was a very good day's work, and no doubt Sir Colin was well satisfied with the deeds of the gallant men under his orders.

The next two days, the 12th and 13th, the Engineers were employed boring their way through the different walls of the palaces and their compounds, which, directly a communication was made, were taken possession of by our troops with but little resistance, the enemy having retired to the line of the Kaiserbagh.

The road from the Begum's palace to the Secunderabagh was open, and I went with Kavanagh to see it and my 53rd friends, who were garrisoning it.

We got a little potted at from the rebel lines, which

were about 300 yards from the road, but without any accident. Our 53rd friends gave us breakfast, after which we went down to the Goomtie to look for a ford, which Kavanagh thought was at the end of the road leading from the Secunderabagh to it, but which we could not find, if it ever existed.

We returned to the batteries near the Begum's palace by another road, through some villages and suburbs, keeping out of sight of the Pandies who had favoured us with their kind attentions.

During the two days that the Engineers were burrowing on, a constant fire of shot and shell was kept up upon the Kaiserbagh and Imaum Barah, and during the afternoon of the 13th the naval guns were got into play upon the latter building within thirty yards of its outer walls, and soon began to make a sensible impression upon it.

At length, on the afternoon of the 14th, the mustering of troops and the yawning appearance of the breach showed that the assault was soon going to take place; and about eleven o'clock the assaulting party was led up by the gallant Major Brasier, with his daring Sikhs, and soon followed by the European regiments under the command of Brigadier Russell of the 84th, the whole operation being under the orders of Brigadier-General Franks.

They soon established themselves in the Imaum Barah, driving all before them out of it and its many and extensive enclosures. We mounted to the top, which was flat-roofed, with balustrades all round, and got a splendid view of the Kaiserbagh and surrounding buildings, and of the enemy flying in all directions. A quantity of sandbags were brought up, and put against the spaces between the balustrades, and some marksmen were established there, who kept up a fire upon any of the enemy who showed themselves. The fire was pretty sharply returned from the loopholes in front of the Kaiserbagh, and from some small guns they had in a battery in front of it.

There were several officers up there, with Colonel Russel, who had been desired by General Franks to remain in observation, and they were mostly sitting down with their backs to the balustrade—smoking their cigars *en attendant* something to do—when a shot came through the wall, and knocked the mortar and dust against Lieutenant Scratchley's (R.E.) back. He never took the cigar out of his mouth, looked coolly round, and picked up the shot, just observing—" Close work this." I never saw any man show more *sang froid* in my life. We could see the Sikhs working gradually on, taking advantage of every piece of cover, and momentarily getting nearer and nearer to the line of the defences of the Kaiserbagh. Presently they made a rush, and, with the 10th, chased the enemy right into their defences, who, taking alarm at the sight of the red and karky jackets, bolted in all directions; and General Franks, following up his success, brought up his troops, and poured them into the squares and enclosures of the Kaiserbagh. Well to the front, with a party of sailors, was Lieutenant Hay, of the *Shannon*, who seized one of the enemy's guns, and turned it upon them with a heavy and destructive fire. Lord Seymour, who was out there as a volunteer, and who was attached to Sir Colin's staff, went back with a note from Brigadier Napier to Sir Colin, acquainting him with our unexpected success. Sir Colin immediately mounted, with his staff, and rode off to the scene of action, ordering up the 84th and other regiments to secure our advantages; and, by the judicious measures which were adopted, all the ground which we had gained was made perfectly safe.

Though the place was now in our possession, yet

from hiding places an occasional fire was kept up, which killed and wounded several officers and men.

Poor Captain Wall, on General Franks' staff, was thus shot dead by his side, while they were sitting together, and thinking matters had become tolerably safe.

Some three hours after the Imaum Barah had been in our possession, as Lord Seymour and I were riding by, two shots came from it, wounding a man. We went in to see if we could dig the hidden Sepoy out, and met Lieutenant Stirling, R.M.A., of the *Shannon*, who immediately brought some of his marines, and searched the place thoroughly, but could find no one but our own camp followers. Either one of them must have fired the shots, or the Sepoy may have escaped as we were riding round to the entrance; anyhow he got off, to our great grief. Of all, what is vulgarly called, the *funky* things, I had any share in, the having to search in dark rooms and holes for a lurking foe, whose eye being accustomed to the *darkness visible* see you perfectly, while you can scarcely discern the hand before your face, is the most so, especially as he is desperate, and like a rat in a corner, is sure to fly at your throat, and the chances are make an end of you before he is himself destroyed. It was thus that poor Hodson lost his life, and several other gallant men also. Lieutenant Stirling, who so gallantly led his men in this search, had been wounded at Kudjra in the leg; but as soon as he could walk, and long before his wound was quite healed, had hurried up to rejoin the force, and resume his share in the duties and dangers of the campaign.

There was not so great a slaughter on this occasion as at the taking of the Begum's palace; for the resistance was not so obstinate, and the Sepoys did not wait to be killed; though to hear their bugling and sounding the advance, one would have thought that they were going to charge us in masses every moment.

About 200 were chased into a building called the "Engine-house," and were killed to a man. Another large body rushed down to the river, but the 23rd, under Colonel Bell (he who captured the first gun at the Alma), were on the look-out, and received them with such a deadly fire from the opposite bank, that they were obliged to fly in another direction, leaving half of their number stretched upon the plain.

Inside the Kaiserbagh there was now immense plundering and looting going on, and in every direction places were found full of valuable property; and if all the reports were true, great quantities of gold and jewels. My only prize was a rather handsome sword, worth two or three pounds at the outside; though, as I was pretty free to go where I liked, I might have got some booty worth having. However, I did not go to India to enrich myself, and therefore did not trouble myself to seek for it.

In one part of the Kaiserbagh were found about forty or fifty women—some of high rank; they were all conveyed to the Martiniere, and made safe and as comfortable as possible—though their jewels were, I am afraid, made safe in another way.

The immense stores of gunpowder found in the cellars and other places in the buildings, made it necessary to be very careful, and to take every precaution; but, in spite of everything, there were several very serious explosions, some of which were attended with the loss of many valuable lives.

It was thought that some were done on purpose by sundry old women who were lurking about, but many of them were evidently accidental. One of the worst, which caused the death of Captain Clarke and Mr. Brownlow, of the Engineers, besides many others killed and wounded, happened while they were throwing a quantity of powder and ammunition down a well, which must have struck something on its way down and exploded, doing all the mischief recounted above.

Sir James Outram was at the same time advancing rapidly on the other side of the Goomtie, and his guns commanded the iron bridge, which he was only waiting till Sir Colin gave the word to take possession of. After the day's work was over I had the pleasure of dining with Sir Colin.

The next day, from the top of the mess-house, which was now General Franks' head-quarters, a large force of the enemy, of all arms, was seen crossing the stone bridge, but in about an hour they were observed returning helter-skelter in the greatest haste and confusion

Jung Bahadour also had an engagement with some of the rebels, and captured several guns, driving them back into their entrenchments. A large force also threatened the Alumbagh, but were repulsed with loss.

I used to go daily, when the work was over, to the Dilkooshah, where Peel was lying wounded, to see him, and some other friends of mine, who unfortunately were also its inmates—for it had been made one of the principal hospitals—Stewart, General Lugard's aide-de-camp, and Major Gloster, of the 38th, who was badly wounded through the stomach, and poor Brockhurst, of the 53rd, who was then thought to be in a fair way of recovery. The Dilkooshah was converted into one of the principal hospitals, and to it were brought the greater part of those who were burnt by explosions, and a wretched state those who were badly burnt were in, their faces being as black as a coal, and so swelled that the features were undistinguishable. The wounds were often dressed with cotton wool, which contrasted fearfully with the deep black of the burnt skin. The smell from them was horrible.

The poor fellows had not much accommodation, for they were laid close together on hospital beds upon the stone floors, which must have been very hard for their poor aching bodies. By far the greater part of those who were badly burned died.

One day Peel asked me whether I thought he was lucky or not in getting wounded. I told him that I thought his reputation was so high and so firmly established, that no casualty like that could add to it, and that it would have been far better for him to have been with his guns in the reduction of Lucknow than lying on a bed of sickness.

On the 17th Sir James Outram took possession of the two bridges, and all the buildings and palaces, including the ruins of the old Residency, the scene of so much suffering and heroism, which line the river from the Kaiser Bagh to the great Imaum Barah, the enemy offering but a feeble resistance, and retreating upon the Mousa Bagh.

On the 19th the Mousa Bagh was attacked, and the enemy were soon driven out of it. Arrangements were made for intercepting their retreat, but, as constantly happens in war, combinations fail, and Brigadier Campbell, from some cause with which I am unacquainted, was not where he was expected to be, and the enemy got off with very little loss.

I had ridden out to see what was going on, and joined Mr. Russell, who was on the same errand, and we arrived at a turning of the road where some of our heavy artillery was halted. The guns were under the command of Lieutenant Warren, R.A.—the same officer who had the breaching-guns at Meangunge in his charge. He told me of a curious defeat he and his gunners had had the day before. Near where they were stationed was a wild-bees' nest, which was unfortunately disturbed; and the enraged insects attacked my friend and his gunners, and stung them so severely, that they were obliged to run off and desert their guns. It would have taken many Sepoys to have effected such a feat. He showed me his head and face covered with stings. We found that without great risk we could not go further, for though our force was considerably in advance of us and of the Mousa Bagh, a great number of the enemy had either doubled back behind them, or had concealed themselves on our advance. The officer commanding a detachment of the 84th, if I remember right, who came back at that time to protect the guns, sent out patrolling and skirmishing parties, and drove out several fellows, hidden near us, who had every inclination to send a ball through any straggler's head who might get inadvertently in their way. While we were staying there an orderly came from the front with some orders, and said he had been shot at sixteen times on the way back;. so we voted that it was not worth the risk, and returned to spend some hours looking over the large Imaum Barah and the other buildings now in our hands.

Among the prizes taken at the Kaiserbagh by the 53rd was a rather curious one—a tame rhinoceros, who was reputed to be a hundred years old; it certainly was nearly blind, and quite stupid, but very good-natured, and would let one pull him by the horn or rub his scaly coat of mail without showing the slightest displeasure. He was taken up to their camp, and when I left them, he was there in safety, and, if not in clover, certainly in the midst of plenty.

On the 21st there was an attempt made to take the Moulvie, who was known to be concealed in the town, but from want of sufficient force to surround him, he escaped, though he was in the house when the troops attacked it. It was a great pity that his capture was not effected, as he is one of our bitterest and most able enemies, and was, by the latest despatches from Rohilcund, leading a powerful, but unfortunately for us, a flying army against us.*

---

* Since killed by a friendly Zemindar.

The Moulvie being driven out of the town might be considered as the finishing stroke to the capture of Lucknow. Sir Colin issued his Order, thanking the army for the exertions and bravery by which it had been effected; and thus closed one act of the mighty drama which is being played over the vast plains of India.

CHAPTER XII.

TURN HOMEWARD — MARCH TO CAWNPORE — LEAVE-TAKING — ARRIVAL AT FUTTEYPORE — ALLAHABAD — LOSE MY CAP — IMPROMPTU ONE — ROBBERY OF MALAKOFF — ARRIVE IN OLD ENGLAND.

As the work seemed for the present nearly over, I began to take counsel with myself what was to be done next. I had some wishes to travel northward, and avoid the heat of the summer in the hill country; but the difficulties and the risks that must be incurred were so much greater in proportion than any pleasure likely to be derived from that course, that I gave it up; and moreover I had a great swelling beneath one of my knees, as big as a hen's egg, which was getting very painful, and which has kept me laid up or on crutches for the last six months, and from which I am only now recovering. I felt that I should be obliged to lay up, and thought it would be no fun following the army in a dhooly; especially that, as soon as an outsider cannot take care of himself, he becomes a nuisance and useless. All these considerations combined, determined me to get home by the overland route as quickly as I could; and as the Naval Brigade were going down country to rejoin the *Shannon*, I bethought myself to march down with them. But their orders were not forthcoming; and on the 23rd I heard that General Franks was going down to Cawnpore that night with a slender escort, so I went over to his quarters, and begged his leave to accompany him there, and take advantage of the protection the Sowars who were to accompany him would afford. It would have been very unwise to have attempted to go by oneself, for after the dispersion of the rebels from Lucknow the roads had become still more unsafe than before, and bodies of them were likely to be met with in every direction. He very kindly gave me leave to do as I requested, and I went off to get my things ready for a start, and to take a hurried leave of my friends, two of whom, alas! are now no more—poor Brockhurst, of the 53rd, and Sir William Peel.

In the death of the latter, the service and his friends have sustained a great loss; his short but brilliant career has been marked by a devotion to his duty—a constantly doing what was right because it was right—always pressing forward in the path of honour, he served his country as she well merits to be served. Brave but humane, daring but forethoughtful, he so perfected the means at his disposal, that when they were brought into the field they were irresistible, and did as much as men and material could do. In action cool, collected, and fearless, he led on his guns, and poured their well-directed fire upon the enemy, encouraging his men by his calm yet earnest manner, utterly regardless of danger, utterly unmoved by the iron storm often raging about him.

Highly educated and talented, a good sailor, a good navigator, with a complete knowledge of his profession, having a thorough acquaintance with its arms, its powers, and its requirements, he was simple and unostentatious in his manner, friendly and conciliatory in his address, upright and honourable in his heart. His life, short as it unfortunately has been, has left behind it one of those beacon-lights of glory, one of those polar stars of honour for future heroes to steer their course by; and his name is added to those of that glorious company so dear to every British heart—the naval heroes of England. I was favoured with his acquaintance and friendship only for the few short months while with the army in India; but they will be always among my dearest recollections as long as memory and life endure.

I was to repair to General Franks' tent at half-past six, and was there, bag and baggage, punctually, but found that he was going to sit down to dinner for the last time with his staff; and he kindly asked me to join, which I was glad to do, for only four hours to take leave of one's friends, pack up one's traps, settle mess accounts, and get ready to leave India for England, did not leave much time for eating, so that I was quite prepared to lay in so good and welcome a store for our night's journey as General Franks' hospitality set before me.

I was not able to take leave of the greater part of my 53rd friends, for they had gone out the day before on an expedition; but it will be long before the recollection of their kindness and goodness to me fades from my recollection. From the time when my dear friend Colonel English took me in tow at Benares, till the time I left Lucknow, to take my departure from India, I received from them all the greatest friendship, hospitality, and consideration; and I trust before very long to meet them again in health and happiness in Old England.

We were to complete the journey to Cawnpore in one march—General Franks, who was unwell, going in a dhooly, and the rest of us riding—our servants and baggage following as quickly as they could. An anecdote I was told of General Franks by one of the officers of the 10th will give as good a picture of the man as volumes could. When he first succeeded to the command of the 10th, some things did not come up to his ideas of efficiency and discipline, and he set to work to correct what he thought wrong in a determined manner; and, as is usually the case when people head back our little pleasant irregularities, he got proportionally abused, and a report got about that some of his men intended to shoot him the first time they went into action. Soon afterwards we had the struggle in the Punjab, and just before going into action he addressed his men, saying—" I hear some of you mean to shoot me; all I can say is, if you fire in the direction I go, you will do no harm;" and so bravely and well did he lead them up to the enemy, that ever since no regiment has been more proud of its colonel than the gallant 10th are of the strict, though undaunted Franks.

We had a safe, though wearisome march as far as Onoa, where we arrived about eight or nine in the morning—(it is no joke riding about forty miles at night at a foot-pace)—and there we found two companies of the 82nd, who took us in and did for us—gave us breakfast and shelter. After resting for a few hours, and having taken good care that my mare should be well fed and cared for, I cantered over to Cawnpore by myself—the General waiting for the cool of the evening—and went to my friend Cannon's, who was hospitality itself, and put me and my horse up.

The next day I was busy selling my horses and what things I did not want on my passage home.

At Cawnpore I met Major Le Mesurier, who had had a narrow escape on his way down with his company of artillery from Lucknow—a large body of some thousand of the enemy having crossed the road between him and his baggage at night. They would have made mince-meat of his hundred men in a quarter less no time.

On the evening of the 26th I left Cawnpore in a dâk carriage, and next morning arrived at Futteypore,

CHANGING HORSES ON THE GRAND TRUNK ROAD

GONE IN THE LOINS

London, Saunders & Otley.

where I put up with my friend, Major Knox Babington, of the 17th Madras Native Infantry, who received me with his wonted kindness.

There I rejoined General Franks, who had come on the day before, and we went on to Allahabad in the train that afternoon.

Soon after the garry started from Cawnpore, soft slumbers stealing over my senses, I got fast wrapped in the arms of Murphy, from whose fond embrace I did not escape till the next morning at daylight; when, on awaking, I discovered that no cap was on my head. I looked everywhere—turned over the luggage, pulled out the cushions, fumbled in the pockets again and again; asked Malakoff for it. "Master have cap on master's head when master go to sleep." It must have tumbled off in the night, and was doubtless many miles astern. "Here's a pretty go!" thought I. I've got no other; a jolly hot Indian sun rising up to broil all day; Messrs. Cater and Co., hat and cap makers to Royalty and to Captain Jones, away some 10,000 or more miles as a crow would fly. Certainly no hat or cap-shop, however humble, nearer than Allahabad! I thought I should be broiled or roasted, or get a *coup de soleil* before I got there! What, indeed, was to be done? I thought of committing highway robbery, and with a revolver in each hand, and a sword between my teeth, demanding of the first *clean*-looking nigger I met his turban or his life. I thought of contriving a turban out of a table-cloth I had (I should have been disappointed there, for my discharged servants had appropriated it). At last it struck me. Hurrah! I've got a spare cap-cover.

Instantly I got it out, together with two towels and a needle and thread from the aforesaid Malakoff, and folding one up pretty thickly, I stitched it into the crown, and folding the other long-ways, sewed it round the inside; and when it was completed, found myself the happy possessor of as sunproof a cap as any man in India, and a very respectable-looking piece of head-gear; indeed, it lasted me to Calcutta, and I had no other when at Allahabad I waited on Lord Canning, who, notwithstanding my rough travelling costume (and people usually get up rather smart when they pay their respects to the Governor-General), received me with that kindness and courteous urbanity which form such pleasing features in the thorough-bred English gentleman, and which he possesses in a remarkable degree.

I had left Malakoff at the station at Futteypore to take care of my things. When I met him there he was looking the picture of despair, and told me that the syces and bheesties, whom I had paid off, with a good tip each, at Cawnpore, had opened his bundle, and stolen all his fine dresses and ornaments, and the things he had picked up at Lucknow. It was a great loss to the poor fellow, and shows in a true light the character of these villanous niggers. A lot of servants, who all, doubtless, had got their share of loot, to rob a fellow-servant of his savings and property, with whom they had been living on good terms for many months!

The railroad had only been opened as far as Futteypore two days before by the Governor-General, and troops had to be stationed along it at different places, as part of the country through which it runs is by no means secure.

At Allahabad we heard of the attack by Koer Sing upon our forces at Azimghur, and that Lord Mark Kerr and the 13th, with a detachment of the Bays, had marched upon Benares, and thence were to proceed to reinforce and relieve the garrison there; and General Franks was asked by the Governor-General to take command of the force. He took me with him, and when we arrived at Benares he began making the necessary dispositions; but a telegraphic order from Sir Colin Campbell arrived for no offensive operations to be undertaken until Sir E. Lugard's arrival with a strong column, which had been sent off from Lucknow, so that General Franks' presence was no longer required; and on the evening of the 30th we left Mr. Gubbins's hospitable house, where we had been entertained, and proceeded by dâk towards Rannee Gunge.

It is to Mr. Gubbins that much of the safety that has been enjoyed at Benares is due; his firmness, and the excellent information which he always possessed, have been of incalculable value. At his house I enjoyed that Indian hospitality so much and so justly vaunted. We arrived at Benares about six in the morning, and went to his house. Franks, who was acquainted with him, said, "Gubbins, I've come with my two aides-de-camp to stay with you for a couple of days." And we were immediately welcomed, and treated *en prince*.

Henry Henderson, of the 10th, one of the best fellows in the world, the General's aide-de-camp, shared his dâk carriage with me, and the General, who is six feet two, and broad-shouldered in proportion, had one to himself.

We travelled all night, and halted from about nine till four or five, during the heat of the day, at the comfortable little rest-houses which are established every twelve miles on the road, and arrived at Rannee Gunge on the 2nd of April, and having got our orders to proceed that night to Calcutta, left by the train at eleven, and arrived early the next morning.

The country which we passed through was generally flattish, and without much feature, except in the neighbourhood of Shergotty, where for some thirty or forty miles it is more varied; and was as deficient in colouring as in diversity of form; the leaves had mostly fallen off, or were a dirty greenish-brown, except where here and there a solitary tree had, anticipating its neighbours, burst out in bright and tender green foliage, or some tree (name to me unknown, botany not being taught at the Royal Naval College) shone forth in the splendour of a scarlet flower, as thick as foliage, but without a green leaf to relieve it, presenting altogether the most unharmonious landscape imaginable. The only thing which can convey an idea of the ugliness of the scenery would be a rather hard neutral tint and sepia drawing, with very bright green and scarlet wafers dotted about it. The golden tints of the glorious East—Bosh!!

I put up at Wilson's comfortable hotel, and soon afterwards called upon my agents, to whom I had written from Lucknow, begging them to secure me a berth in the next packet to England, and found that they had succeeded in doing so, which was a great piece of luck, for at that time of the year the berths were generally secured for months previously.

On the 10th of April we left India in the Peninsular and Oriental ship *Indus*. Among my fellow-passengers I met several old friends and acquaintances going home—Franks, and his aide-de-camp Henderson, Brigadier Russell, Captain Steele, 9th Lancers, who was fast recovering from his severe wounds received at Shumshabad; Captain Probyn, now Major, C.B., and V.C.; —— Wake, the magistrate, and gallant defender of Arrah; Lord Seymour, mentioned for his gallantry at the relief of Lucknow by Sir Colin Campbell; Patrick Stewart, the indefatigable officer who had had charge of the telegraph at head-quarters; Sir Archdale Wilson, the conqueror of Delhi, and Mr. Edwards and his faithful Sikh servant, whose adventures and escape have made so interesting a narrative.

At the relief of Lucknow Brigadier Russell had the most wonderful escape. A cannon-ball just grazed his neck, and cutting his shirt-collar and a little gold chain in two, hardly raised the skin; however, he was paralysed for some time, but in a day was quite well again.

I took Malakoff with me as far as Madras, and when I discharged him, made up to him partly his losses stolen from him by his rascally fellow-servants. He was going on foot to Hyderabad, and had the consolation of knowing, as he told me, that there were *plenty tiger, plenty loot waller, plenty bud mashes* on the way.

We had a splendid and prosperous passage to Suez; and while at Cairo had time to visit the Fort, Mosque, and to see the Mamaluke's Leap, a marvellous drop of forty or fifty feet. How he or his horse could survive is most wonderful.

On our arrival at Alexandria we found that we had some hours to spare, so Swiney and I got a carriage, and drove to see the lions, the afore-mentioned Bump his belly—Pompey's Pillar; Pattle's sneeres—Cleopatra's Needle, &c.; then returned to the hotel, where the greater part of our fellow-passengers were assembled to have an early dinner at the *table d'hôte*. The conversation turned upon the Egyptian plan of hatching eggs in ovens; and one of our friends, learned in the law, and a sharp fellow too, remarked, "Well, one good thing is, that as the eggs are hatched in this artificial manner, there can be no occasion for cocks and hens in Egypt." I took the liberty of suggesting to him that the hens might be wanted to *lay* the eggs, and that the cocks might be useful, too, as there would not be much chance of the hens laying very many eggs, unless, as Betsey Austen, of Barbadian renown, would say—"The cock him make lub to um hen!"

I had taken my passage to Southampton, but as those among my fellow-passengers with whom I was most intimate were going *viâ* Marseilles, I altered my line of route, and joined a party consisting of Major Steele, Probyn, J. Clayton, Swiney, a young officer of the Bengal Light Cavalry, and an American gentleman, and a very pleasant companion.

At Malta we heard that there was a very bad feeling on the part of the French for us, on account of the acquittal of Dr. Bernard, and we rather expected that something disagreeable might occur; but, on the contrary, nothing could be pleasanter than everything was during our "trajet" through France.

We stayed two days at Paris, and admired the wonderful improvements which Louis Napoleon has spread over it.

On Monday, the 17th of May, we left Paris, taking the route of Boulogne and Folkestone, and arrived in England, I having been absent little more than seven months, but they had been seven months of much interest and adventure, the excitement of which made one enjoy with more zest the quiet of home, and the domestic pleasures of Old England.

THE END.

www.ingramcontent.com/pod-product-compliance
Lightning Source LLC
Chambersburg PA
CBHW060502090426
42735CB00011B/2080